M000158213

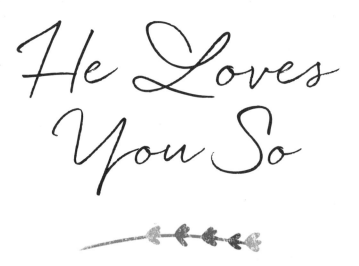

He Loves You So

FALLING DEEPER INTO GOD'S HEART: A 366-DAY DEVOTIONAL

Chosen

a division of Baker Publishing Group
Minneapolis, Minnesota

© 2022 by Baker Publishing Group

Published by Chosen Books
11400 Hampshire Avenue South
Bloomington, Minnesota 55438
www.chosenbooks.com

Chosen Books is a division of
Baker Publishing Group, Grand Rapids, Michigan

Printed in China

ISBN 978-0-8007-6235-3 (cloth)
ISBN 978-1-4934-3585-2 (ebook)

Library of Congress Control Number: 2021023555

Written by Stephany Dawn Pracht

Cover design by Studio Gearbox

Baker Publishing Group publications use paper produced from sustainable forestry practices and post-consumer waste whenever possible.

22 23 24 25 26 27 28   7 6 5 4 3 2 1

Introduction

> Look with wonder at the depth of the Father's marvelous love that he has lavished on us! He has called us and made us his very own beloved children.
>
> 1 JOHN 3:1 TPT

Do you ever wonder if God has a list of favorites? And if He did, might it not be possible that His daily walks in the Garden of Eden with Adam and Eve would be on such a list? He created them, in His image, to have fellowship with Him, every day. He left heaven daily to come spend time with them. Lavish love, indeed!

Those daily visits ended when Adam and Eve fell into sin as the beguiling serpent questioned God's love and care for them. The redemption of mankind would take some time, but thankfully, God had a plan all along. A plan that shouts louder than our past, a plan that shouts we are precious in God's sight.

You are so precious, in fact, that God sent His Son, Jesus Christ, for you. The price of sinfulness was paid in full, the record of our sins washed away by the blood of Jesus. The pathway to reestablish relationship with Him, the Creator of heaven and earth, has been blown wide open.

He Loves You So is your invitation to walk daily with your heavenly Father. The readings are in biblical order, based on the featured Scripture verse. As you walk daily with God, you will also walk through the Bible during the year. As you spend time with Him, lean in and hear His tender, reassuring voice. A voice that will offer you comfort, joy, courage, direction and peace.

> The same way a loving father feels toward his children—that's but a sample of your tender feelings toward us, your beloved children, who live in awe of you.
>
> Psalm 103:13 TPT

Set aside those few moments each day to take in these simple, practical, biblical, Spirit-led reminders of how very precious and valuable you are.

. . . Because He loves you so!

The Law

Then God said, "Let us make man in our image, after our likeness."

GENESIS 1:26

PRAY

Father God, King Jesus and the Holy Spirit, I am fearfully and wonderfully made in Your beautiful image. Inhabit and strengthen me to bear and mirror Your image well. Do not let me settle for imitating someone else's reflection of You. I was not made in their secondhand image. I was created to carry and proclaim Your magnificent image. Thank You, Lord!

DECLARE

I am uniquely created in God's image,
so others may see Him in me!

He loves you so!

So God created man in his own image, in the image of
God he created him; male and female he created them.

GENESIS 1:27

PRAY

*Father God, Creator of all, You took the time
to mold and form humans in Your own image
and breathed the breath of life into us. We are
all Your image-bearers. Please help me not to
forget the affection, purpose, creativity and love
that shape me, my family, friends, co-workers,
classmates, neighbors and "enemies." Give me
eyes to see everyone as You created them, and
give me a heart to love each person as You do.
Thank You, Lord!*

DECLARE

I have God's eyes to see the image of
God in those around me!

He loves you so!

≡ But Noah found favor in the eyes of the LORD.

GENESIS 6:8

PRAY

Amazing Lord, Your sweet gaze is upon me. Thank You that I have found favor in Your eyes and that Your favor rests on me. I pray that Your favor opens up floodgates of ways to know You and experience You more. May Your favor shine on me and cause me to overflow with joy in Your magnificent Presence. Thank You, Lord!

DECLARE

God's favor rests on me and works through me!

He loves you so!

And he was afraid and said, "How awesome is this place! This is none other than the house of God, and this is the gate of heaven."

GENESIS 28:17

PRAY

Almighty Lord God, You do not live in man-made buildings of mere stone and wood—they cannot contain Your greatness. You choose to live in the hearts and lives of all who love You. And, oh, how I love You. Thank You for making Your home in me. Show me how to live as Your gate of heaven on earth. Thank You, Lord!

DECLARE

I am God's dwelling place—His tabernacle—today!

He loves you so!

"As for you, you meant evil against me, but God meant it for good, to bring it about that many people should be kept alive, as they are today."

GENESIS 50:20

PRAY

Almighty God, I praise You for Your power and eagerness to redeem even the darkest moments of my life. There is nothing that You cannot restore and redeem for my greater good. Your zeal declares that You are working Your life-fulfilling purposes for me. You are moving for my greatest good all the time. Display Your glory! Thank You, Lord!

DECLARE

My pain can be transformed to bring God glory!

He loves you so!

God said to Moses, "I AM WHO I AM." And he said, "Say this to the people of Israel: 'I AM has sent me to you.'"

EXODUS 3:14

PRAY

Lord God, You are the I Am Who I Am! The Great I Am! The Eternal One! You were before the creation of all that there is. You are from everlasting to everlasting! You are who You say You are, always! I praise You that You never change. As Moses could depend on You, so can I. Thank You, Lord!

DECLARE

My God is the Great I Am, and He has chosen
to send me to proclaim His name!

He loves you so!

Then the LORD said to him, "Who has made man's mouth? Who makes him mute, or deaf, or seeing, or blind? Is it not I, the LORD?"

EXODUS 4:11

PRAY

Precious Lord, You are Creator, Master, Savior, Healer, Provider and Defender. You are all these things and so much more. You alone are worthy of my total faith, trust and obedience. You are so faithful and true. Work through me all of my days as You will. I am Your arms, Your feet, Your words. I am Your vessel. Thank You, Lord!

DECLARE

However I view God, I am prepared to look even higher!

He loves you so!

"Now therefore go, and I will be with your mouth and teach you what you shall speak."

EXODUS 4:12

PRAY

Almighty Lord, forgive me for postponing obedience as I wrestle to understand. I know I don't need to understand before I obey. But You also know I struggle in my desire to understand first and obey second. Make me step quickly when You direct, even if I do not see the next step. Help me not to focus on my perceived inabilities, but to focus on You. Thank You, Lord!

DECLARE

My understanding is not a requirement
before obeying God!

He loves you so!

Say therefore to the people of Israel, "I am the LORD, and I will bring you out from under the burdens of the Egyptians, and I will deliver you from slavery to them, and I will redeem you with an outstretched arm and with great acts of judgment."

EXODUS 6:6

PRAY

God, with Your mighty, outstretched arm, You always accomplish what You say You will do. You are the "I will" God! For all Your children, You have prepared a banquet table in the presence of our/Your enemies to display that You are the God who does exceedingly, abundantly, beyond. Impossible and unbelievable are normal for You! Please show me Your glory! Thank You, Lord!

DECLARE

I live in the shadow and the power of the "I will" God!

He loves you so!

"Lift up your staff, and stretch out your hand over the sea and divide it, that the people of Israel may go through the sea on dry ground."

EXODUS 14:16

PRAY

Lord God, I desire to vividly experience Your working and moving in impossible situations in my life, encountering You in every part of my life. I pray for bold and victorious faith. Stretch my boundaries; lead me to step out and follow You. You will never let me down! You will make a way! All things are possible for You! Thank You, Lord!

DECLARE

Impossible victories are the way of
life with my Almighty God!

He loves you so!

The LORD used to speak to Moses face to face, as a man speaks to his friend.

EXODUS 33:11

PRAY

Abba Father, in Your Word You tell me that You now call me friend. A friend of God! In that friendship, I know You desire to intimately talk with me. Help me to push away distractions and busyness to hear You speak. Help me to move from You being just a part of my life, to You being my life. Consume me, my Friend! Thank You, Lord!

DECLARE

God, who knows me fully and
completely, calls me His friend!

He loves you so!

"Now therefore, if I have found favor in your sight, please show me now your ways, that I may know you in order to find favor in your sight. Consider too that this nation is your people."

EXODUS 33:13

PRAY

Lord, Your extravagant favor flows over and through me. I boldly come before You; show me now Your ways. Give me ears to hear Your voice and eyes to see You working and moving in and around me. May my heart always be hungry to know You—to know who You are and what You are like. Thank You, Lord!

DECLARE

I have God's favor on me to know
Him, His will and His ways!

He loves you so!

And he said, "My presence will go with you, and I will give you rest."

EXODUS 33:14

PRAY

Father God, I know that peace is not merely the absence of a raging storm. Perfect peace is clinging to Your Presence while going through the crashing waves, experiencing that peace that passes all understanding. God of all peace, teach me to breathe deeply Your refreshing breath of life, to lean into Your Presence and truly rest. Thank You, Lord!

DECLARE

God's Presence is sweet peace that shelters my soul!

He loves you so!

Moses said, "Please show me your glory."

EXODUS 33:18

PRAY

Abba Father, I cry out like Moses—show me Your glory! Lift me to higher levels of experiencing You. I want to uncover a deeper truth and knowledge of You. I want my love for You to grow more and more. I pray for such an intimacy with You that I can pass Your truth along to the next generation so that they can go higher and deeper with You. Thank You, Lord!

DECLARE

The height of my intimacy with God will
be the floor of future generations!

He loves you so!

"But from there you will seek the LORD your God and you will find him, if you search after him with all your heart and with all your soul."

DEUTERONOMY 4:29

PRAY

Father God, You are not hiding from me. You are waiting for me to lift my eyes to You. Position me to gaze on Your beauty. Place me in the perfect spot so that You can lavishly fill my heart with You—Your love, mercy and grace—so much so that You overflow from me onto each person I meet. Thank You, Lord!

DECLARE

God is not hiding from me—He wants me
to seek Him and embrace Him!

He loves you so!

And you said, "Behold, the LORD our God has shown us his glory and greatness, and we have heard his voice out of the midst of the fire. This day we have seen God speak with man, and man still live."

DEUTERONOMY 5:24

PRAY

Jesus, thank You for becoming flesh and living on this earth so that I can behold Your glory. Open my eyes so that I have an unobstructed view of You. I want to see Your wonder and praise You more. I want to grasp more of Your holiness so that I will fall before You in humble, abandoned worship. I want my heart to be awed, over and over again, by Your beauty, love and grace—to be Your glory-bearer! Thank You, Lord!

DECLARE

I am God's image and glory-bearer on the earth!

He loves you so!

You shall write them on the doorposts of your house and on your gates.

DEUTERONOMY 6:9

PRAY

Lord God, Your Word is meant to surround me. As I go out and come in, I need it to cover me like the blood on the doorposts during Passover. I need You and Your Word of truth always before me. I pray You will be conspicuously alive and active in and through me. Help me to make my first reaction for You and Your way. Thank You, Lord!

DECLARE

The Word of God drenches me, surrounding me!

He loves you so!

"For you are a people holy to the LORD your God. The LORD your God has chosen you to be a people for his treasured possession, out of all the peoples who are on the face of the earth."

DEUTERONOMY 7:6

PRAY

Lord, help me today to grasp more thoroughly and more intimately how precious I am to You. I am Your treasure, not because of who I am or anything I have done, but because of who You are. By Your undeserved favor, You have chosen me to be holy unto You, a sacred vessel to be used for Your glory. Thank You, Lord!

DECLARE

I am God's chosen, holy and treasured possession!

He loves you so!

He is your praise and He is your God, who has done these great and awesome things for you which your eyes have seen.

DEUTERONOMY 10:21 NASB 1995

PRAY

Abba Father, may I be filled with the wonder and belief of Mary. The vision and obedience of Joseph. The joy and celebration of the angels. The awe and eagerness of the shepherds. The determination and discernment of the wise men. The darkness-piercing brilliance of the star. And the perfect peace of the Prince of Peace. Thank You, Lord!

DECLARE

The Holy Spirit floods my daily life with awe and wonder!

He loves you so!

For the LORD your God is he who goes with you to fight
for you against your enemies, to give you the victory.

DEUTERONOMY 20:4

PRAY

All-powerful and Almighty God, You not only walk with me into my battles, but You lead the way. You are always victoriously fighting every battle for me. You thwart every battle plan the enemy sets up against me. You have made me an overcomer. You bring the victory as I trust in You alone. You are my Victory! Thank You, Lord!

DECLARE

God is for me! God is fighting for me!

He loves you so!

"Be strong and courageous. Do not fear or be in dread of them, for it is the LORD your God who goes with you. He will not leave you or forsake you."

DEUTERONOMY 31:6

PRAY

God, unless Your Presence goes with me, I am totally lost. Thank You for the promise that You are always with me. You will never leave me. Engrave the promise on my heart so that I can go forward strong and courageous, with no fear or dread of any obstacle that may try to get in the way. Hand in hand with You, I am equipped and empowered for anything that comes my way. Thank You, Lord!

DECLARE

God's Presence will never leave me—
He surrounds me everywhere I go!

He loves you so!

"It is the LORD who goes before you. He will be with you; he will not leave you or forsake you. Do not fear or be dismayed."

DEUTERONOMY 31:8

PRAY

Abba Father, what a most wonderful promise! It is genuinely overwhelming to know that You will never leave me, that You can never fail me. You are preparing the way in front of me. You are behind me, guarding my back. You walk with me each step of the way. Thank You for always being my Sustainer, my Shelter, my Strength, my Song. Thank You, Lord!

DECLARE

God goes before me, making my way straight. He will always be with me!

He loves you so!

History

"Have I not commanded you? Be strong and courageous. Do not be frightened, and do not be dismayed, for the LORD your God is with you wherever you go."

JOSHUA 1:9

PRAY

Abba Father, You have commanded that I be strong and courageous. I have no need to worry or be anxious because You are with me wherever I go. You have called me to stand firm in Your strength. Your presence is a promise, a treasure and a joy. Help me to go forward without fear, never overwhelmed by any circumstances I may face. Thank You, Lord!

DECLARE

I am strong and courageous because God's Presence is with me everywhere I go!

He loves you so!

"And when they make a long blast with the ram's horn, when you hear the sound of the trumpet, then all the people shall shout with a great shout, and the wall of the city will fall down flat, and the people shall go up, everyone straight before him."

JOSHUA 6:5

PRAY

King Jesus, thank You that You position me for greater triumphs, for bigger victories. As You direct, I will purposefully and passionately keep marching, keep serving, keep worshiping and keep following You in total triumph. I will listen and obey until You cause every wall to fall. Let my shouts of praise be heard around the world! Thank You, Lord!

DECLARE

I live my life from a place of victory
because of Jesus' triumph!

He loves you so!

But the LORD said to Samuel, "Do not look on his appearance or on the height of his stature, because I have rejected him. For the LORD sees not as man sees: man looks on the outward appearance, but the LORD looks on the heart."

1 SAMUEL 16:7

PRAY

Lord God, You see beyond what I can see. I am grateful that You look past all my perceived flaws to gaze on the beauty You created in me. Your eyes go beyond all my weaknesses, shortcomings and failures and see my heart. I am blessed that when You see me, You say that I am good. Help me to do the same with others. Thank You, Lord!

DECLARE

God knows and sees who He created
me to be—the real me!

He loves you so!

Then Samuel took the horn of oil and anointed him in the midst of his brothers. And the Spirit of the LORD rushed upon David from that day forward.

1 SAMUEL 16:13

PRAY

Dear Lord, thank You that You created and called me for Your eternal purpose. During the routines of daily life, help me to see and know that You are using my ordinary todays to prepare me for what You have planned for all my extraordinary tomorrows. You have blessed me to be a blessing that is irrevocable. Thank You, Lord!

DECLARE

God has called and gifted me for His purpose, and He will not take it back!

He loves you so!

David danced before the LORD with all his might.

2 SAMUEL 6:14

PRAY

Awesome Lord, worthy are You. I want to worship You extravagantly, just as David did, unconcerned about what others think or say about me. Dancing in abandon to the melody of Your glorious praise. Singing in harmony with the chorus of heaven. Please give me the courage to unapologetically live a life of extravagant worship before You. Thank You, Lord!

DECLARE

Exuberant and extravagant worship is my
natural response to God's goodness!

He loves you so!

He said, "The LORD is my rock and my fortress and my deliverer."

2 SAMUEL 22:2

PRAY

Lord God, You alone are my Rock, my Strong Tower, my Fortress and my Deliverer. In You, I will not be shaken or overtaken. I will praise and dance before You in joyous celebration of Your mighty work in me. Whenever things get shaky, help me remember that it is on Christ, the solid Rock, I stand. Thank You, Lord!

DECLARE

I am hidden in the cleft of the Rock!

He loves you so!

"And you call upon the name of your god, and I will call upon the name of the LORD, and the God who answers by fire, he is God." And all the people answered, "It is well spoken."

1 KINGS 18:24

PRAY

Lord God, You know all there is to know. You know all the battles before me. You know what I need before I know how to ask. Help me to seek You more than any gifts or answers. Make Yourself known in mighty ways in my battles so that others have no doubt that You are God. Thank You, Lord!

DECLARE

God will fight my battles with His mighty fire!

He loves you so!

Then Elisha prayed and said, "O Lord, please open his eyes that he may see." So the Lord opened the eyes of the young man, and he saw, and behold, the mountain was full of horses and chariots of fire all around Elisha.

2 Kings 6:17

PRAY

Commanding Lord, I cry out to You. Please rip in two the veil that separates Your visible and invisible kingdom. Open my eyes that I may see Your mighty army taking ranks. Open my eyes so that I can join You in making the way for Your will to be done on earth as it is in heaven. Thank You, Lord!

DECLARE

I see with the eyes of faith the army of the Lord!

He loves you so!

"So now, O LORD our God, save us, please, from his hand, that all the kingdoms of the earth may know that you, O LORD, are God alone."

2 KINGS 19:19

PRAY

Father God, You have set the stage for a miraculous and mighty deliverance on my behalf. The enemy has never been a match for You. You boldly honor Your children who have patiently waited on You to move. You have beautifully orchestrated the redemption of the time the enemy has stolen so that those around can know that You alone are God. Thank You, Lord!

DECLARE

God is doing miraculous and mighty things,
and the world will know He is God!

He loves you so!

Jabez called upon the God of Israel, saying, "Oh that you would bless me and enlarge my border, and that your hand might be with me, and that you would keep me from harm so that it might not bring me pain!" And God granted what he asked.

1 CHRONICLES 4:10

PRAY

Lord, I pray for the courage not to limit You and not to be reluctant to ask You to pour out Your blessings. My asking and receiving does not keep someone else's prayers from being answered. You are enough for all. You are always more than enough. I pray today for breakthrough in my emotions, relationships, finances and influence. Thank You, Lord!

DECLARE

God is expanding and enlarging my
sphere of favor and influence!

He loves you so!

Oh give thanks to the LORD, for he is good; for his steadfast love endures forever!

1 CHRONICLES 16:34

PRAY

Abba Daddy, I will follow You no matter what. Wherever You lead me, I am not afraid to be called extravagant or excessive in my worship of You or in my relationship with You. Your steadfast, unfailing love has birthed more beauty into my life than I ever dared to dream of or hope for. Thank You, Lord!

DECLARE

I will thank the Lord for His goodness
and steadfast, immovable love!

He loves you so!

"Give me now wisdom and knowledge to go out and come in before this people, for who can govern this people of yours, which is so great?"

2 CHRONICLES 1:10

PRAY

Lord, You have promised that if I lack wisdom, I should ask You to give it and believe that I can receive it. So here I am. Open my heart and mind to Your perfect knowledge, truth and wisdom. May my decisions be flooded with Your light, knowledge and justice. Those things will enable me to do all the things You ask me to do, especially those that are far greater than I ever imagined. Thank You, Lord!

DECLARE

God delights to reveal His wisdom and knowledge to me!

He loves you so!

"If my people who are called by my name humble themselves, and pray and seek my face and turn from their wicked ways, then I will hear from heaven and will forgive their sin and heal their land."

2 CHRONICLES 7:14

PRAY

Almighty God, help me to grasp that corporate revival begins with my own personal, individual revival, when You light me on fire for You. Holy Spirit, work through me, to help me to humble myself and pray in Spirit and in truth, to turn from my own wicked ways and seek Your face. Thank You for hearing me, forgiving me and bringing healing to my heart. Thank You, Lord!

DECLARE

True, real and lasting revival starts in me!

He loves you so!

For the eyes of the LORD run to and fro throughout the whole earth, to give strong support to those whose heart is blameless toward him.

2 CHRONICLES 16:9

PRAY

Lord, You are the God who sees me. I pray to have a heart that is completely and fully devoted to You. I surrender every corner of my life, every moment of my day, to You. I choose to live in trust and confidence in You and Your Word. Holy Spirit, I invite You to consume every part of me. Thank You, Lord!

DECLARE

I am living delightfully and joyfully blameless before God!

He loves you so!

"You are the LORD, you alone. You have made heaven, the heaven of heavens, with all their host, the earth and all that is on it, the seas and all that is in them; and you preserve all of them; and the host of heaven worships you."

NEHEMIAH 9:6

PRAY

Lord, You alone are God! You are huge! You are bigger than my mind can comprehend. You are more than able! You are more than willing! You are working and moving in my life today! No matter how much I know of You, there are still vast oceans more to learn. You are my life, and my life is in Your hands! Thank You, Lord!

DECLARE

The Lord, the Creator of all, is actively working and moving in my life every day!

He loves you so!

"For if you keep silent at this time, relief and deliverance will rise for the Jews from another place, but you and your father's house will perish. And who knows whether you have not come to the kingdom for such a time as this?"

ESTHER 4:14

PRAY

Lord God Almighty, it is so exciting to be alive at this precise time in history. You intentionally created me for such a time as this. You purposefully placed me here at this exact moment. You are working Your divine purpose through me today. Help me to make the most of my time, abilities, gifts and resources purposed in me for this time. Thank You, Lord!

DECLARE

This moment in history is my "such a time as this"!

He loves you so!

For I know that my Redeemer lives, and at the last he will stand upon the earth.

JOB 19:25

PRAY

Father God, thank You that Jesus is my Redeemer and that He lives! Jesus, You are the Lamb destined to be slain before the creation of the world. You are the Faithful Witness. You are the Lion of Judah. You are the Conquering King. In triumph You are seated on Your throne, but soon You will again stand on the earth! You alone are worthy! Thank You, Lord!

DECLARE

My Redeemer lives, and He will return for me!

He loves you so!

"I have not departed from the commandment of his lips; I have treasured the words of his mouth more than my portion of food."

JOB 23:12

PRAY

Almighty Lord, give me a holy hunger for Your Word. Help me to cling tightly to Your Word of Life. Fill my heart and mind with Your discernment and understanding so that I can walk in step with You each moment. I pray that Your truths will shine light in and through me every moment of the day. Thank You, Lord!

DECLARE

God's perfect Word is alive and active in and through me!

He loves you so!

"For he looks to the ends of the earth and sees everything under the heavens."

JOB 28:24

PRAY

Sovereign Lord, You alone are over all that exists. You see everything here on the earth. You see my future because You have written it all in Your book. Help me to live this day the way You see it, trusting You with the things beyond my vision, as well as those things I think I see clearly. Thank You, Lord!

DECLARE

God sees every detail of my life, and
I am divinely led by Him!

He loves you so!

"I know that you can do all things; no purpose of yours can be thwarted."

JOB 42:2 NIV

PRAY

Lord, I declare that no matter how much I may kick and scream or how much the world doubts and denies or how much the enemy tries to distract and destroy—Your plans cannot be stopped! You can do all things! You are who You say You are! You do what You say You will do! You are the unstoppable God! Thank You, Lord!

DECLARE

I am following hard after the Unstoppable God!

He loves you so!

Poetry

But you, O LORD, are a shield about me, my glory, and the lifter of my head.

PSALM 3:3

PRAY

Lord God, Your Presence and precious love is like a shield that surrounds me and protects me. I love that! You are my Glory as Your divine favor rests on me. You are the Giver of love and the Lifter of my head. I never need to be ashamed as I snuggle close to You, secure in Your presence. Thank You, Lord!

DECLARE

God is my Shield and the Lifter of my head!

He loves you so!

I have set the LORD always before me; because he is at my
right hand, I shall not be shaken.

PSALM 16:8

PRAY

*Abba Father, teach me how to always set You
before me so that I see things from Your per-
spective. Cause me to see through eyes of faith
in who You are. Help me to remember that You
are beside me and that nothing need shake my
faith in You. Teach me how to live each day more
closely with You and more intimately connected
to You. Thank You, Lord!*

DECLARE

The Lord is with me, always by my side.
I will not be shaken!

He loves you so!

You make known to me the path of life. Abundance of joys are in Your presence, eternal pleasures at Your right hand.

PSALM 16:11 TLV

PRAY

Father God, You continually shine Your brilliant light, revealing and illuminating the path of life You have chosen for me. I want to fully embrace Your lasting delight, joy and hope, savoring and resting in Your perfect love. I will cling to Your Presence so that I can become a stronghold of joy and a fortress of hope. Thank You, Lord!

DECLARE

I walk daily in His path of life, where joy overflows!

He loves you so!

≡ I love you, O LORD, my strength.

PSALM 18:1

PRAY

Lord, I love You! I love You because You are so worthy of my love. I love You because You are always faithful. I love You because You are always with me and You strengthen me for this day. I love You because You sent Jesus to pay the price for me to be Your child. I love You because You first loved me. Thank You, Lord!

DECLARE

I will love my Father, who gives me strength for the day!

He loves you so!

You have given me the shield of your salvation, and your right hand supported me, and your gentleness made me great.

PSALM 18:35

PRAY

Lord God, You are so gentle, kind and long-suffering. Let my life and actions echo the gentleness that can only come from You. Just as You support me, help me to lavish support on others. Make me a true reflection of You who is always gentle, supportive and kind. May I be one who points others to You. Thank You, Lord!

DECLARE

I reflect the gentle character, support and lavish kindness of the Prince of Peace!

He loves you so!

Some trust in chariots and some in horses, but we trust in the name of the LORD our God.

PSALM 20:7

PRAY

Abba Father, thank You that You are always faithful and trustworthy. You want me to cry out to You whenever I am in trouble or pain. Thank You for Your name, which is true and faithful. Your name is the only name by which I am saved. I trust completely in Your love and goodness toward me. Thank You, Lord!

DECLARE

I choose to trust in the name of Jesus!

He loves you so!

You prepare a table before me in the presence of my en-emies; you anoint my head with oil; my cup overflows.

PSALM 23:5

PRAY

Lord God, thank You that You have put the enemy under my feet. You have anointed me and given me authority over him, in Jesus' name. No matter what the future holds, You promise to work all of it together for my good. In audacious, over-flowing confidence, I declare that the enemy is defeated, in Jesus' name! Thank You, Lord!

DECLARE

I audaciously sit in the presence of my enemy at the table God has prepared!

He loves you so!

I remain confident of this: I will see the goodness of the LORD in the land of the living.

PSALM 27:13 NIV

PRAY

Creator God, You set the galaxies in place and spun the world into motion. You have witnessed the rise and fall of many peoples and kingdoms. You are from eternity past to eternity future. My life is just one brief moment on Your timeline, but You care to lavish Your love and goodness on me. No matter what tomorrow holds, please reveal more of Your goodness to me today. Thank You, Lord!

DECLARE

God has His goodness in store for me today!

He loves you so!

The LORD is my strength and my shield; in him my heart trusts, and I am helped; my heart exults, and with my song I give thanks to him.

PSALM 28:7

PRAY

Lord, I am helpless on my own, but my heart looks to You, my Strength and my Shield. Empower me with Your strength through the Holy Spirit, not to live in the past but to be ready to embrace the future You have for me. Fill me with Your song of thankfulness as I learn to live in Your freedom. Thank You, Lord!

DECLARE

My heart sings for joy in God's Presence!

He loves you so!

≡ But I trust in you, O LORD; I say, "You are my God."

PSALM 31:14

PRAY

Abba Father, I lift my hands high, praising You.
You are the Lord God Almighty! You are the First
and the Last. Thank You that I can come to You
with all my worries and leave them in Your hands.
I trust in Your unfailing grace and love. Help me
to proclaim with boldness that You alone are my
God. Thank You, Lord!

DECLARE

My God, He alone is God, and I will
have no other gods before Him!

He loves you so!

☰ Commit your way to the LORD; trust in him, and he will act.

PSALM 37:5

PRAY

God, You know that things can spin out of control in an instant. One phone call or email and life is never the same. Help me not to fret over the small details or the big things of my life, but instead to daily commit my way to You. Help me to stop worry the moment it attempts to loudly suggest that You are not trustworthy. You have all the details of my life taken care of! Thank You, Lord!

DECLARE

I commit to walk in the way of the Lord,
and I trust Him to act on my behalf!

He loves you so!

But the meek shall inherit the land and delight themselves in abundant peace.

PSALM 37:11

PRAY

Lord God, I choose to trust You with the circumstances of my today and all of my tomorrows. I will no longer kick and scream due to what I perceive as unfairness in my life. Instead, I will do my best to walk courageously in meekness down every path You lead me on. Fill my heart and mind with Your peace. Thank You, Lord!

DECLARE

Meekness is the strength of God overtaking my heart!

He loves you so!

As the deer pants for streams of water, so my soul pants for you, my God.

PSALM 42:1 NIV

PRAY

Precious Lord, my God, I am desperate for You. As I pour out my heart and my soul to You, help me to realize that You are greater than my failures. You are mightier than all my fears. Help me to boldly face all that today holds. I thank You and praise You for all You are and for all You do. Thank You, Lord!

DECLARE

God will boldly overflow my life with hope, joy and peace!

He loves you so!

Be still, and know that I am God. I will be exalted among the nations, I will be exalted in the earth!

PSALM 46:10

PRAY

Almighty Lord, You are God. Help me learn to be still in Your presence instead of striving and struggling to get things done. As I grow in faith and trust in You, show me how to live in a place of rest, soaking in Your Presence and saturated in Your love as I watch You reveal Your glory. Thank You, Lord!

DECLARE

My way of life is being still and knowing God!

He loves you so!

Cast your burden on the LORD, and he will sustain you; he will never permit the righteous to be moved.

PSALM 55:22

PRAY

Lord of all grace, You have made every provision for me to live today in victory and in Your righteousness. You have lifted all the weight off my shoulders and lightened the load I carry. When the way gets hard, remind me to cast the load onto You, for You will sustain me. I choose to live today trusting in You and Your Spirit to guide and strengthen me. Thank You, Lord!

DECLARE

I cast all my cares on the Lord, who cares for me!

He loves you so!

O God, you are my God; earnestly I seek you; my soul thirsts for you; my flesh faints for you, as in a dry and weary land where there is no water.

PSALM 63:1

PRAY

Lord God, quench my thirst and revive me as my heart and my flesh cry out for You. I desperately need the deep refreshment of Your overflowing, living water. As I travel on the paths that lead through the dry and parched wilderness, only You can quench my deep thirst, for only in You is found the Living Water. Thank You, Lord!

DECLARE

God is my Source of eternal, living water!

He loves you so!

For you, O God, have tested us; you have tried us as silver is tried.

PSALM 66:10

PRAY

Lord God, You are my diligent Refiner. Refined silver reflects the image of the refiner. Please purify and refine me so that it is Your reflection that shines. Continue to gently work out the impurities, rough edges and messy places in my heart. Thank You for Your refining fire. I so want to clearly reveal the beauty of Your glory. Thank You, Lord!

DECLARE

God is refining me to be a reflection
of God's beauty and glory!

He loves you so!

But praises rise to God, for he paid attention to my prayer and answered my cry to him!

PSALM 66:19 TPT

PRAY

Lord God, who hears me, thank You that You are not waiting for me to reach some level of achievement before my prayers can reach You. You delight to hear my prayers with me being just the way that I am. I pray to be Your vessel to reveal Your answer to someone's prayer today. You are the God who hears! You are the God who answers! Thank You, Lord!

DECLARE

God pays close attention to my prayers—He loves to answer me!

He loves you so!

Lord Almighty, you are the one who created all the nations; Look at them—they're all on their way! Yes, the day will come when they all will worship you and put your glory on display.

PSALM 86:9 TPT

PRAY

Abba Father, You so love Your whole creation that You sent Jesus. I pray that in unity all Your children declare and live out Your Kingdom come; that Your will be done on earth as it is in heaven; and that every nation, tribe and tongue begin singing Your anthem: "Salvation belongs to our God who sits on the throne, and to the Lamb!" (Revelation 7:10). Thank You, Lord!

DECLARE

I am a living declaration that God's Kingdom has come!

He loves you so!

I give thanks to you, O Lord my God, with my whole heart, and I will glorify your name forever. For great is your steadfast love toward me.

PSALM 86:12–13

PRAY

Almighty Lord, You want me to live in the truth and reality of Your constant love. You want me to understand the depth, breadth and height of that love and then to accept and receive it with every ounce of me. Demolish any stronghold that is holding me back so that I can continually live in Your extravagant love! Thank You, Lord!

DECLARE

I am lavishly and extravagantly loved by the King of kings!

He loves you so!

So teach us to number our days that we may get a heart of wisdom.

PSALM 90:12

PRAY

Tender Creator, You planned all my days before I breathed my first breath. Help me to be sensitive to Your Spirit leading and guiding me so that I gain wisdom rather than being obsessed with my own to-do list and priorities. Open my eyes to the work—the calling for which You have created me and prepared me. Thank You, Lord!

DECLARE

Every one of my days is important and
to be lived with intentionality!

He loves you so!

Let this be recorded for a generation to come, so that a people yet to be created may praise the LORD.

PSALM 102:18

PRAY

Lord, I pray to live my life in celebration and honor of You. I pray to live a life that matters beyond the moment. A life that speaks Your life for others to see, hear and read. A life that writes a You-story for people now and in the future so that they would know, believe and understand that You alone are God. Thank You, Lord!

DECLARE

God is forging a heritage of faith through me!

He loves you so!

As far as the east is from the west, so far does he remove our transgressions from us.

PSALM 103:12

PRAY

Promise-keeping Lord, You have sworn that You have removed my transgressions "as far as the east is from the west." I choose to take You at Your Word and humbly receive Your costly gift. I accept Your truth and ignore and refute any false sense of guilt. I choose to live in the joy of Your Presence. Thank You, Lord!

DECLARE

I do not get what I rightly deserve; I am given what I could never deserve on my own!

He loves you so!

Our God is in the heavens; he does all that he pleases.

PSALM 115:3

PRAY

Lord, thank You that who You are never changes. You are God! Who You are is infinite! You do whatever You want. Help me never to put You in a box. Keep me from thinking I know how You will always move and work. I accept Your invitation to know and experience You more. Be unrestrained in my life. Thank You, Lord!

DECLARE

God lives unrestrained in and through my heart and life!

He loves you so!

Teach me good judgment and knowledge, for I believe in your commandments.

PSALM 119:66

PRAY

Lord God, Your Word is the only real Truth. It is Your way. It is Your will. Your commandments are my lifeline and my secure anchor. Help me to be discerning and to read between the lines of what people are saying to hear Your truth and knowledge about decisions I face today and every day. Thank You, Lord!

DECLARE

I believe God's Word, and I am learning good judgment and knowledge!

He loves you so!

Blessed is everyone who fears the LORD, who walks in his ways!

PSALM 128:1

PRAY

Holy and righteous God, do not let me be deceived by the world's cheap imitations of peace and happiness. The things of this world can never truly bring lasting joy or satisfy. Lead me, instead, to Your true blessings, to Your abundant and lasting peace. May I overflow with joy as I walk hand in hand with You. Thank You, Lord!

DECLARE

I walk in step with the only true Joy Giver!

He loves you so!

To him who led his people through the wilderness, for his steadfast love endures forever.

PSALM 136:16

PRAY

Father God, I declare that the wilderness will not last. All desert wanderings will come to an end. Your love outlasts all the problems of this life. Your love is more consuming than daily struggles. Your love cannot and will not be stopped. Your love brings incredible beauty out of my imperfect life. Bring on more of Your beauty! Thank You, Lord!

DECLARE

God is lavishing perfect love through my imperfections!

He loves you so!

He's the God who chose us when we were nothing! His tender love for us continues on forever!

PSALM 136:23 TPT

PRAY

Abba Father, I give thanks to You. You are good. You are God of all gods! You are Lord of lords! You came down and scooped me up when I was lost and miserable, and You poured your tender love on me. I will cling to You, the God of all mercy and grace and comfort. Your great love endures forever. Thank You, Lord!

DECLARE

He chose me, and His love is with me forever!

He loves you so!

You hem me in, behind and before, and lay your hand upon me.

PSALM 139:5

PRAY

Father God, thank You for the precious knowledge that Your hand is upon me. I sense the gentle weight of Your touch on my life. Wherever I go, You lead me and guard me. I am hidden securely in the palm of Your hand. I thank You for all the ways You are present in my life. You defend, preserve and protect me. Thank You, Lord!

DECLARE

God has chosen to put His hand upon
my life, to keep me in all my ways.

He loves you so!

You formed my innermost being, shaping my delicate inside and my intricate outside, and wove them all together in my mother's womb.

PSALM 139:13 TPT

PRAY

Yahweh, I am the stone; You are the Sculptor. I am the clay; You are the Potter. I am the instrument; You are the Composer—the Musician. I am the canvas; You are the Painter—the Master Artist. You are the Breath of Life. May every beat of my heart and every fiber of my being seek to love You with the same consuming passion with which You love me. Thank You, Lord!

DECLARE

I am a masterpiece, created by the hand of God!

He loves you so!

I praise you, for I am fearfully and wonderfully made.
Wonderful are your works; my soul knows it very well.

PSALM 139:14

PRAY

Abba Father, Creator, all Your works are wonderful—and that includes me! I am fearfully and wonderfully made in Your beautiful image. I am uniquely created to reflect Your Presence and splendor. Your glory flows and is released through me. Loose me from anything that binds me so I can be the original and unique person You intended me to be. Thank You, Lord!

DECLARE

As God's creation, I am fearfully and wonderfully made, with His intent in mind!

He loves you so!

Search me, O God, and know my heart! Try me and know my thoughts!

PSALM 139:23

PRAY

Lord God, it is so reassuring to know that You are not finished with me yet. You know me better than I know myself. Please search my heart and show me any way that I have left my first love. Help me get rid of thoughts or habits in my life that hinder and harm our relationship. Thank You, Lord!

DECLARE

God is not through with me! He is perfecting me!

He loves you so!

They shall pour forth the fame of your abundant goodness and shall sing aloud of your righteousness.

PSALM 145:7

PRAY

Lord Almighty, Yours is the greatness and the power and the glory and the majesty and the splendor, for everything in heaven and earth is Yours. It is all Your creation. You are greater than all. You do whatever You please. You are righteous and perfect in all Your ways. You are loving to all You have made. Thank You, Lord!

DECLARE

I unapologetically tell others of Your abundant goodness and righteousness!

He loves you so!

He fulfills the desire of those who fear him; he also hears their cry and saves them.

PSALM 145:19

PRAY

Sweet Lord, open my heart to see any way in which I have been attempting to be in control, attempting to accomplish something only You can do. Help me to cease trying to run my own life. You always hear and respond to the cries of my heart. As I cry out to You, You will completely satisfy. Thank You, Lord!

DECLARE

God hears me and satisfies my heart's cry!

He loves you so!

≡ Praise the LORD! Praise the LORD, O my soul!

PSALM 146:1

PRAY

Abba Father, thank You for each time You surprise me with circumstances turning out better than I could ever hope for or imagine. Help me to learn that I can trust Your goodness to work things out for my good every time. You know more and better than me every single time. I invite You to surprise me with Your extreme goodness today. Thank You, Lord!

DECLARE

I will praise the Lord because His goodness
is continually poured out over my life!

He loves you so!

≡ He heals the wounds of every shattered heart.

PSALM 147:3 TPT

PRAY

Father God, living in this world is full of bumps and bruises. Unplanned heartbreaks and sickness loom around every corner. So many are seeking health and wellness in all the wrong places. You alone are the Healer. In this day and time, You are able and willing and eager to heal all brokenness and bind up all wounds. Thank You, Lord!

DECLARE

God is willing and able to heal today—both body and soul!

He loves you so!

How great is our God! There's absolutely nothing his power cannot accomplish, and he has infinite understanding of everything.

PSALM 147:5 TPT

PRAY

Lord God, my finite understanding struggles even to begin to grasp how huge You are. As I raise my hands and lift my eyes to You, drench me in a delightful downpour of Your Presence. I can only release what I have received. Saturate me with all that You are. I need more of Your power flowing through me. Thank You, Lord!

DECLARE

My God is a great God, and His power
can accomplish anything!

He loves you so!

Trust in the LORD with all your heart, and do not lean on your own understanding.

PROVERBS 3:5

PRAY

Father God, I only see part of the picture. You see it all. You know it all. Help me to focus completely on You, not on the circumstances that surround me. Hold my gaze in the palms of Your hands. Build my trust in You and Your ways, and help me to shy away from handling things through my limited understanding. Thank You, Lord!

DECLARE

My heart trusts in God completely, causing my own human understanding to take a back seat!

He loves you so!

> But the path of the righteous is like the light of dawn,
> which shines brighter and brighter until full day.

PROVERBS 4:18

PRAY

Father of Light, breaking through the darkness is Your specialty. My path is made brilliant with Your light. Holy Spirit, shine brightly in and through me so that all I do illuminates the darkness around me. May I be a child of light who brings honor, glory and praise to Jesus—who is the Light of the world. Thank You, Lord!

DECLARE

God's light illuminates my path so I can walk in safety, peace, hope, love, mercy and grace!

He loves you so!

Set your gaze on the path before you. With fixed purpose, looking straight ahead, ignore life's distractions.

PROVERBS 4:25 TPT

PRAY

Lord, life can be so crazy and unpredictable. But You are never shocked or shaken. When distractions do come creeping into my life, cause me to stop and immediately bring You into the situation, so that Your Presence can transform it into an opportunity to glorify You. I pray that I stay continually and intentionally focused on You. Thank You, Lord!

DECLARE

I focus my mind and heart on the love, mercy, grace and joy that God lavishes on me!

He loves you so!

There is one whose rash words are like sword thrusts, but the tongue of the wise brings healing.

PROVERBS 12:18

PRAY

Precious Lord, I pray that I will be quick to listen and slow to speak. Keep me from responding from pure emotion. Help me to always listen for Your gentle whisper that gives me words to say. Fill me to overflowing with Your wisdom and discernment so that I am able to readily speak Your words that bring healing and life. Thank You, Lord!

DECLARE

I am filled to overflowing with God's healing words!

He loves you so!

What has been is what will be, and what has been done is what will be done, and there is nothing new under the sun.

ECCLESIASTES 1:9

PRAY

Lord, remind me, deep within my spirit, that You have been faithful to do it before and You will do it again! You have healed me. You have opened my prison doors and broken off my chains. You have brought restoration and redemption. More than once, You have made a way where there seemed to be no way. Remind me that You will do it again! You will never fail me! You are always with me! Thank You, Lord!

DECLARE

My God has done it before, and He will do it again!

He loves you so!

He brought me to the banqueting house, and his banner over me was love.

SONG OF SOLOMON 2:4

PRAY

Almighty God, You invite me into Your very Presence, where You have fullness of joy ready and waiting for me, where You provide true nourishment for my soul. It delights Your heart to have me with You, for us to spend time together. You enjoy seeing me smile and laugh. You keep me under Your banner of love! Thank You, Lord!

DECLARE

God loves me so! Say that again: GOD LOVES ME SO!

He loves you so!

Set me as a seal upon your heart, as a seal upon your arm, for love is strong as death, jealousy is fierce as the grave. Its flashes are flashes of fire, the very flame of the LORD.

SONG OF SOLOMON 8:6

PRAY

Abba Father, be the seal engraved upon my heart as it burns with love for You. Hedge me in so that if I begin to wander, Your jealous love flashes before my eyes and draws me back to You. With my heart reserved and sealed for You, lead me to live each moment confidently and boldly in Your love alone. Thank You, Lord!

DECLARE

God is the seal set upon my heart!

He loves you so!

Prophecy

In the year that King Uzziah died I saw the Lord sitting upon a throne, high and lifted up; and the train of his robe filled the temple.

ISAIAH 6:1

PRAY

Almighty Lord, You are always seated on Your heavenly throne. Your glory, that which You are clothed in, fills me, Your temple. I will never exhaust discovering all there is to know about You. There is so much more of You than I can imagine. My deep desire is to know and experience You more today! Give me eyes to see You high and lifted up! Thank You, Lord!

DECLARE

The King who sits on the throne will show me more of Himself today!

He loves you so!

Then I heard the Lord saying, "Whom should I send to my people? Who will go to represent us?" I spoke up and said, "I will be the one. Send me."

ISAIAH 6:8 TPT

PRAY

Lord God, thank You that You are not looking for the wisest or the most talented people to work through. But You are seeking out the willing and available. I make myself always available to You, to be useful to You in whatever ways You see fit. I cry out to You—here I am, send me! Thank You, Lord!

DECLARE

I will be the one—God's one! Send me!

He loves you so!

The LORD of hosts has sworn: "As I have planned, so shall it be, and as I have purposed, so shall it stand."

ISAIAH 14:24

PRAY

Abba Father, the world screams to be fearful and afraid, but Your Word confidently and boldly proclaims that You have a plan for good. What You have determined will come about. There is nothing and no one that can stand in the way of Your purposes. You promise that You are working out Your good plans for my life! Thank You, Lord!

DECLARE

I am confident that Almighty God is orchestrating His good plans for me!

He loves you so!

You keep him in perfect peace whose mind is stayed on you, because he trusts in you.

ISAIAH 26:3

PRAY

Abba Father, You alone are perfect peace. Help me to keep my eyes fixed on You and to have faith and trust in You more fully. Fill my thoughts with Your glory, goodness, wonder and peace. Give me fresh eyes as I read the Word so that I see more of You. Take my breath away with You! Thank You, Lord!

DECLARE

My mind is focused on the King of glory!

He loves you so!

"And now, go, write it before them on a tablet and inscribe it in a book, that it may be for the time to come as a witness forever."

ISAIAH 30:8

PRAY

Lord, I am awed that You want me to be a part of Your plan and purpose. You have something to accomplish through me today that will impact history. May I proclaim Your story, which You have written through me, so that others encounter Your love. So that even future generations can see You, know You and love You. Thank You, Lord!

DECLARE

God speaks His words—His story—boldly through me!

He loves you so!

And your ears shall hear a word behind you, saying, "This is the way, walk in it," when you turn to the right or when you turn to the left.

ISAIAH 30:21

PRAY

Lord God, You are the whisper in my ear. I desire to hear clearly what You speak to me. Unclog my ears from anything that hinders me from hearing You. You clearly say the most loving, fruitful and exciting words, guiding me in what I should know and do. May I hear Your gentle voice telling me the way. Thank You, Lord!

DECLARE

I discern the living, active voice of God!

He loves you so!

Have you not known? Have you not heard? The LORD is the everlasting God, the Creator of the ends of the earth. He does not faint or grow weary; his understanding is unsearchable. He gives power to the faint, and to him who has no might he increases strength.

ISAIAH 40:28–29

PRAY

Father, You are the Creator and Architect of every detail of my life. Please grow in me unshakeable, immovable, abundant faith in Your love and Your promises that do not faint or grow weary. When fear, anxiety and confusion come, give me Your power and might to increase my strength to stand in You, my unshakeable, immovable, abundant Abba Father! Thank You, Lord!

DECLARE

Daily abundance of power and strength are mine! Abundance is my inheritance!

He loves you so!

He empowers the feeble and infuses the powerless with increasing strength.

ISAIAH 40:29 TPT

PRAY

Lord, I declare that in You I am strong. There is no pit too deep that You cannot rescue me from it. There is no captive You cannot set free. There is no sickness, no disease, You cannot heal. There is no person You cannot save. There is no brokenness You cannot bind up. There is no sin You cannot forgive. Help me to be strong in You as You strengthen me with Your Spirit. Thank You, God!

DECLARE

God empowers me with all strength and might!

He loves you so!

They who wait for the LORD shall renew their strength; they shall mount up with wings like eagles; they shall run and not be weary; they shall walk and not faint.

ISAIAH 40:31

PRAY

Abba Father, sometimes this journey of life seems long and very tiring. I admit that today, exhaustion feels like it has overtaken me. But You are always faithful. You promise that if I wait on You, You will renew my strength—strength to run and not grow weary, to walk in Your ways and not faint. In faith, help me to put one foot in front of the other and to experience Your renewal. Thank You, Lord!

DECLARE

God supplies the renewed energy and strength
I need to keep moving forward!

He loves you so!

"For I, the LORD your God, hold your right hand; it is I who say to you, 'Fear not, I am the one who helps you.'"

ISAIAH 41:13

PRAY

Lord God, You are a gentle and kind Father who reaches down to tenderly care for me. You care so deeply that You hold my hand as You wrap me in Your safety and gently guide me on my path. Remind me to lean into You and lift my eyes to You. You are my Help. I have no fear! Thank You, Lord!

DECLARE

I am secure in the gentle grip of the Everlasting Lord!

He loves you so!

But now thus says the LORD, he who created you, O Jacob, he who formed you, O Israel: "Fear not, for I have redeemed you; I have called you by name, you are mine."

ISAIAH 43:1

PRAY

Lord God Almighty, You are the One who stretched out the expanse of the heavens and beyond, because Your word is that powerful. And yet You know me by name, just like Moses, Samuel and David—WOW! You care to take the time to bend down to know me. You care about me. You are redeeming everything that concerns me. I am Yours! Thank You, Lord!

DECLARE

God cares about me, and He knows me by name!

He loves you so!

All the nations gather together, and the peoples assemble. Who among them can declare this, and show us the former things? Let them bring their witnesses to prove them right, and let them hear and say, It is true.

ISAIAH 43:9

PRAY

Almighty God, You are on Your throne. You are over all there is. How I pray that others see Your truth living in and through me. I pray that my actions declare that You alone are God, and if need be, that my words do as well. Leave no doubt that You alone are God so that others say, "It is true!" Thank You, Lord!

DECLARE

My life declares that it is true! My God is alive!

He loves you so!

"You are my witnesses," declares the LORD, "and my servant whom I have chosen, that you may know and believe me and understand that I am he. Before me no god was formed, nor shall there be any after me."

ISAIAH 43:10

PRAY

Lord God, there is no other god before You. There is no other god but You. You have declared that I am Your set-apart witness and Your chosen servant. Help me to boldly live out Your declarations about me. You have chosen me to know You, believe You and understand that You are the Great I Am. Thank You, Lord!

DECLARE

I am the chosen witness and servant of the Great I Am!

He loves you so!

I am doing something brand new, something unheard of. Even now it sprouts and grows and matures. Don't you perceive it? I will make a way in the wilderness and open up flowing streams in the desert.

ISAIAH 43:19 TPT

PRAY

Abba Father, open my eyes to see clearly the brand-new things that You are doing. Open my ears to hear Your gentle whisper, urging me to come to where You are. I want to more than grasp the new things You are doing; I want to take my place in releasing the reality of Your love and Your Presence on the earth. Thank You, Lord!

DECLARE

I am an essential part of the new thing God is doing!

He loves you so!

You will neither have to leave in haste, nor will you make a frantic escape, for your God, Yahweh, will go before you. He will lead you each step and be your rear guard.

ISAIAH 52:12 TPT

PRAY

Commander of the Angel Armies, I proclaim that You have got this! No matter what it is, You are in control. There is no need to worry or be anxious. You have made a way where there seems to be no way before. I declare that You will do it again! You have my back! You are the Way Maker! Thank You, Lord!

DECLARE

God goes before me! God comes behind me! God walks with me!

He loves you so!

"Increase is coming, so enlarge your tent and add extensions to your dwelling. Hold nothing back! Make the tent ropes longer and the pegs stronger."

ISAIAH 54:2 TPT

PRAY

Almighty Lord, I want more of You! I need more of You! I have only started to glimpse how awesome and mighty You are. I am hungry to know You deeper, to see You in all truth and glory, and to be filled to overflowing with Your perfect love. Stretch me to live outside the box with You. Thank You, Lord!

DECLARE

I have only just begun to know and experience
the increase the Lord has for me!

He loves you so!

"For as the heavens are higher than the earth, so are my ways higher than your ways and my thoughts than your thoughts."

ISAIAH 55:9

PRAY

Lord God, I know that Your thoughts are far higher than mine. Your ways are far better than mine. I will not pretend to understand why You have allowed some things in my life, but I choose to trust You, Your ways, Your good purposes and the love and beauty You want to bring. You are always good! Thank You, Lord!

DECLARE

God's higher plan for me is good and trustworthy!

He loves you so!

"These I will bring to my holy mountain, and make them joyful in my house of prayer; their burnt offerings and their sacrifices will be accepted on my altar; for my house shall be called a house of prayer for all peoples."

ISAIAH 56:7

PRAY

Lord, make me Your house of prayer—joyfully celebrating You, crying out to You for my family, my friends, my city, my state, my country, my world . . . for mountains to move! Help me to remember that the power of prayer is never found in my words, but is found in You . . . the One who hears from heaven. You, Lord, are bigger, greater and always with me. Thank You, Lord!

DECLARE

I am God's beautiful and powerful house of prayer!

He loves you so!

Behold, the LORD's hand is not shortened, that it cannot save, or his ear dull, that it cannot hear.

ISAIAH 59:1

PRAY

Lord, at times I need to know that You see me specifically, that You hear my cries and that You are moved to action on my behalf. You are orchestrating and setting the stage for the unbelievable, the impossible, to happen. You will leave no doubt that You are on Your throne. Your children have Your full attention, and only You are mighty to save! Thank You, Lord!

DECLARE

God knows my voice individually, specifically and intimately!

He loves you so!

"Arise, shine, for your light has come, and the glory of the LORD has risen upon you."

ISAIAH 60:1

PRAY

Father God, because the Light of the World lives inside of me through the Holy Spirit, it is possible for me to shine Your light wherever I go. Please help me remember that I am a city on a hill. I am a light to be displayed, not to be hidden under a basket. Your Presence fills me so that Your Light shines out into the dark world around me! Thank You, Lord!

DECLARE

God's light shines through me to dispel all darkness!

He loves you so!

The Spirit of the Lord GOD is upon me, because the LORD has anointed me to bring good news to the poor; he has sent me to bind up the brokenhearted, to proclaim liberty to the captives, and the opening of the prison to those who are bound.

ISAIAH 61:1

PRAY

Lord God, You have poured out Your Holy Spirit on me and given me my marching orders. I pray to live a life that proclaims the true liberty found in You, to be Your balm to bring healing to the hurting and broken and to fling wide the gates of Your freedom to everyone who is bound. Thank You, Lord!

DECLARE

The Spirit of the Lord God is upon me!

He loves you so!

To proclaim the year of the LORD's favor, and the day of vengeance of our God; to comfort all who mourn.

ISAIAH 61:2

PRAY

Lord God, my life is safe in Your hands. Nowhere else would I be more positioned for blessing, peace, joy and favor. May each step I take today and every day proclaim Your Presence, igniting in all the people I encounter a burning desire to know and encounter You. I pray that Your love through me would comfort others. Thank You, Lord!

DECLARE

I will proclaim the Lord's favor and
bring comfort to others!

He loves you so!

From of old no one has heard or perceived by the ear, no eye has seen a God besides you, who acts for those who wait for him.

ISAIAH 64:4

PRAY

Abba Father, hinder me and keep me from underestimating all that You have in store for me. Stop any and all disbelief regarding Your generosity and blessings. Empower me through Your Holy Spirit to anticipate huge and mighty things from You because You are the God who does exceedingly, abundantly beyond anything I can even dare to dream. Thank You, Lord!

DECLARE

My Abba Father knows how to give great gifts!

He loves you so!

Thus says the LORD: "Heaven is my throne, and the earth is my footstool; what is the house that you would build for me, and what is the place of my rest?"

ISAIAH 66:1

PRAY

Father God, so much of the time, life just does not make sense to me. Teach me what You want me to change by praying, by declaring or by obedient action. Guide me to step out in faith knowing that everything and anything overwhelming to me or over my head is securely under Your feet! Thank You, Lord!

DECLARE

Any of my overwhelming situations is nothing for my God!

He loves you so!

"Before I formed you in the womb I knew you, and before you were born I consecrated you."

JEREMIAH 1:5

PRAY

Father, I love only because You loved me first. I did not choose You first, but You chose me. You wanted me, and You sought me out. Help me to live perpetually in the truth and understanding that You chose me. I am accepted and never left out. You have loved me, and You knew me from the foundation of time. Thank You, Lord!

DECLARE

God chose me! God continually chooses me every day!

He loves you so!

Heal me, O LORD, and I shall be healed; save me, and I shall be saved, for you are my praise.

JEREMIAH 17:14

PRAY

Lord of all, I believe that You have the power to heal any and all of the wounds of my body and my spirit. You came down and made a way to save me from my lost and wandering ways, and I am saved. Let my words always praise You for all You have done, for what You are doing today and for what You will do. Thank You, Lord!

DECLARE

God is Jehovah Rapha, my Healer and my Savior!

He loves you so!

"Is not My word like fire?" declares the LORD, "and like a hammer which shatters a rock?"

JEREMIAH 23:29 NASB 1995

PRAY

Abba Father, I ask that through the power of Your Word and the reality of Your truth, You would shatter all the lies that haunt me and bind me. Call to mind that they are rubble and dust. Send Your Word as fire to burn down every false thought. Let the fire of Your Word ignite revival in me. Thank You, Lord!

DECLARE

God's Word is the fire that burns
away any lies I have believed!

He loves you so!

"For I know the plans I have for you," declares the LORD, "plans for welfare and not for evil, to give you a future and a hope."

JEREMIAH 29:11

PRAY

Wonderful Lord, You are the covenant-keeping God. You have promised and declared that You have a good plan for me. You are working out and giving me an amazing future that stomps out all evil and is abundant, filled with hope and promise. Use this covenant promise to set me free to trust in Your plans for my life. Thank You, Lord!

DECLARE

I confidently and boldly move forward
because God has a good plan for me!

He loves you so!

"Then you will call upon me and come and pray to me, and I will hear you."

JEREMIAH 29:12

PRAY

Lord, the fact that You, the God of the universe, hear me whenever I call causes me to fall to my knees in worship. I can ask with confident expectation and the assurance of faith. You know exactly where I am and where I am going. You are taking me from glory to glory, day by day, leading me in Your divine plan. You are working everything out for my good and Your glory. Thank You, Lord!

DECLARE

God always hears and responds to
my prayers—to my voice!

He loves you so!

The LORD appeared to him from far away. I have loved you with an everlasting love; therefore I have continued my faithfulness to you.

JEREMIAH 31:3

PRAY

Abba Father, thank You for loving me with a love that can never run out or dry up. May Your love saturate every part of me—spirit, soul, mind and body. I cry out to encounter and experience Your love in deeper ways than I have ever known before. I long to truly grasp how wide, how long, how high and how deep Your love is. Thank You, Lord!

DECLARE

God's love saturates every part of my heart and soul!

He loves you so!

Ah, Lord GOD! It is you who have made the heavens and the earth by your great power and by your outstretched arm! Nothing is too hard for you.

JEREMIAH 32:17

PRAY

Elohim, the Mighty One, the impossible is where You are just getting started. Your power is unending. You create something out of nothing. You mold the new thing in the palm of Your hand. You transform the ordinary into the extraordinary. Making impossibilities possible is Your specialty. You make a way where there seems to be no way—today! Thank You, Lord!

DECLARE

God's power and strength are for my good!

He loves you so!

"Behold, I am the LORD, the God of all flesh. Is anything too hard for me?"

JEREMIAH 32:27

PRAY

Lord God, You are the God of all, and there is nothing that is too hard for You. That truth is far beyond my understanding. Help me to believe! Hinder my natural reaction of putting You in a box or keeping You there. I long to see Your power at work because You do exceedingly, abundantly beyond all that I can even picture. Thank You, Lord!

DECLARE

There are no limits on what my God can do!

He loves you so!

"Call to me and I will answer you, and will tell you great and hidden things that you have not known."

JEREMIAH 33:3

PRAY

Lord God, as I spend time in Your Presence, You open up and reveal Your eternal plans and Your divine strategies to me. You want to talk to me and discuss things with me even more than I know. Thank You that You want me to hear Your voice and that You give me the ability to hear You. Thank You, Lord!

DECLARE

God wants me to hear His voice! My ears
hear and know the voice of God!

He loves you so!

"And I will put my Spirit within you, and cause you to walk in my statutes and be careful to obey my rules."

EZEKIEL 36:27

PRAY

Almighty Lord, guard my steps so that I may not grieve Your Spirit by walking in the flesh. Protect my mind from harmful or vain thoughts that waste and squander too many moments. Never let me take Your grace for granted, but help me to remember that it came at a high price—the blood of Jesus, Your precious Son. Thank You, Lord!

DECLARE

God's Holy Spirit lives in and through me!

He loves you so!

How great are his signs, how mighty his wonders! His kingdom is an everlasting kingdom, and his dominion endures from generation to generation.

DANIEL 4:3

PRAY

King of Glory, You are from everlasting to everlasting. There is no beginning or end to You. You always have been, and You always will be. You are unending. Holy Spirit, breathe into my heart Your pure and heavenly desires. Let Your truth permeate my mind and thoughts. Grant me eyes of faith to see Your signs and wonders. Thank You, Lord!

DECLARE

The Holy Spirit reveals His amazing wonders to me!

He loves you so!

"I will restore to you the years that the swarming locust has eaten, the hopper, the destroyer, and the cutter, my great army, which I sent among you."

JOEL 2:25

PRAY

Redeeming Lord, You know and have seen all that has happened in my life. You know how the enemy has tried to steal, kill and destroy in my history. I pray that You restore to me anything and everything that has been wrecked. Redeem and restore every single bit of it. Fill me with fresh joy and the realization of all You died to save me from and for. Thank You, Lord!

DECLARE

God is restoring and redeeming all for me!

He loves you so!

"And it shall come to pass afterward, that I will pour out my Spirit on all flesh; your sons and your daughters shall prophesy, your old men shall dream dreams, and your young men shall see visions."

JOEL 2:28

PRAY

Everlasting Lord, You see everything from beginning to end. There is nothing that You miss. You are working Your plan and vision for this world. Help me take steps to see Your vision happen. Give me divine and simple strategies that set goals and plans so that I know where I am going and how You want me to get there. Thank You, Lord!

DECLARE

God gives me dreams and visions to declare to others!

He loves you so!

Write the vision; make it plain on tablets, so he may run who reads it.

HABAKKUK 2:2

PRAY

Lord, Your Word is not complicated or stale. Your truth is vibrant and alive and active for people today. For such a time as this, write Your story on my heart and in my mind, and give me the courage to share it from my lips. Proclaim Your truth through me, so that others see and know how great, mighty and awesome You are. Thank You, Lord!

DECLARE

God gives me His words to proclaim for this time!

He loves you so!

Behold, his soul is puffed up; it is not upright within him,
but the righteous shall live by his faith.

HABAKKUK 2:4

PRAY

Lord God, please help me to live today recognizing that You are in control of every situation I face. When I am tempted to take off on my own whims, pull me back, close to You. Help me to intentionally place my life completely in Your hands and live in faith. Keep me on a short leash. Thank You, Lord!

DECLARE

Living by faith, in the shadow of the
Most High, is my safe place!

He loves you so!

For the earth will be filled with the knowledge of the glory of the LORD as the waters cover the sea.

HABAKKUK 2:14

PRAY

King Jesus, I say, "Yes! Come on!" to Your glory filling the earth. Flood the world with Your awesome presence. I want to be Your vessel, filled with Your glory, which You can pour out whenever it is needed. Show me today what I can do to flood my home, my city and the world with Your Presence and glory. Thank You, Lord!

DECLARE

Yes, come, King Jesus. Fill the earth with Your glory!

He loves you so!

O LORD, I have heard the report of you, and your work, O LORD, do I fear. In the midst of the years revive it; in the midst of the years make it known; in wrath remember mercy.

HABAKKUK 3:2

PRAY

Almighty Lord, I have heard the wonderful stories of Your strong and powerful arm. I have read of Your glorious and mighty works. I stand in awe of all that You are and all You have done. I know You are not done yet. Invade my life with Your awesome Presence. I want to know the One True God more deeply. Thank You, Lord!

DECLARE

God is revealing more of Himself to me!

He loves you so!

GOD, the Lord, is my strength; he makes my feet like the deer's; he makes me tread on my high places.

HABAKKUK 3:19

PRAY

Almighty God, You are my strength! Because of You, I am secure and can walk through the tight places. In You, those tight places become wide-open spaces. You cause me to traverse higher grounds as I go deeper with You. Help me to actively live in Your strength with sure steps that cause me to walk in breakthrough, restoration and redemption. Thank You, Lord!

DECLARE

God calls me to walk higher with Him, and
He gives me the strength to do it!

He loves you so!

The LORD your God is in your midst, a mighty one who will save; he will rejoice over you with gladness; he will quiet you by his love; he will exult over you with loud singing.

ZEPHANIAH 3:17

PRAY

Abba Daddy, just the thought that You are always with me and that You rejoice over me as Your precious child causes my heart to sing. And You sing over me with joy! I am both humbled and overwhelmed. My heart feels like it might explode. Teach me to live in the way that always delights and honors. Thank You, Lord!

DECLARE

God rejoices and sings love songs over me!

He loves you so!

Then he said to me, "This is the word of the LORD to Zerubbabel: Not by might, nor by power, but by my Spirit, says the LORD of hosts."

ZECHARIAH 4:6

PRAY

Lord, thank You that I do not have to be strong enough or smart enough on my own, because I am just not. What a relief to know it is through Your strength, might and power that I can do all things. Holy Spirit, be released to equip and empower me to do all I have been created and called to do. Thank You, Lord!

DECLARE

I am equipped and empowered to accomplish all that I am called to do by the Presence of the Holy Spirit!

He loves you so!

"For from the rising of the sun to its setting my name will be great among the nations, and in every place incense will be offered to my name, and a pure offering. For my name will be great among the nations," says the LORD of hosts.

MALACHI 1:11

PRAY

Abba Father, empower and strengthen me in this moment and time to proclaim Your greatness. I desire to be the extravagant display and demonstration of who You are and how great You are so that every nation, tribe and tongue will know that You alone are God. You are the King of kings, the Lord of lords, the Lover of their souls! I say, "Yes, Lord, Your great name alone is worthy!" Thank You, Lord!

DECLARE

I am a bold explosion to make God's name known, as His Spirit lives in and through me!

He loves you so!

"But for you who fear my name, the sun of righteousness shall rise with healing in its wings. You shall go out leaping like calves from the stall."

MALACHI 4:2

PRAY

Lord, Your name is great and is to be praised and revered. Teach me to always honor Your name and to walk in awe of who You are. Please bring healing to my life and joy to my walk. Let Your extravagant grace overflow through me as I receive Your healing. Let my joy and delight be uncontained. Thank You, Lord!

DECLARE

As the Son brings healing, I will go out
rejoicing and telling others!

He loves you so!

Gospels

> Then suddenly the voice of the Father shouted from the sky, saying, "This is the Son I love, and my greatest delight is in him."

MATTHEW 3:17 TPT

PRAY

Abba Father, my desire is to love Your Son as You did. I want to shout it so others hear! So often, though, I am quiet and look for delight in other people or things. Please forgive me. Guide me to walk in full dependence on the power and guidance of the Holy Spirit, as I delight myself in You. Thank You, Lord!

DECLARE

I delight in God, my Savior, and His Son, Jesus Christ!

He loves you so!

"Blessed are those who mourn, for they shall be comforted."

MATTHEW 5:4

PRAY

Father, in this world filled with trouble and sin, it would be easy to become hardened because of the pain in my heart. As I mourn, please keep my heart tender to Your comfort. Help the rhythm of my heart to beat with Yours. Then, as I am comforted, may I share that comfort with those around me. Thank You, Lord!

DECLARE

My God comforts me in my pain and sadness!

He loves you so!

"Blessed are those who hunger and thirst for righteousness, for they shall be satisfied."

MATTHEW 5:6

PRAY

Christ Jesus, give me a longing for Your satisfying righteousness. Grow in my heart the desire to live out Your righteousness in my daily moments. Forgive me for seeking fulfillment in things that can never fulfill me. Fill me with a hunger and thirst that can only be satisfied by the One who knows me so well. Thank You, Lord!

DECLARE

In Christ alone, I find my hunger and
thirst for righteousness fulfilled!

He loves you so!

"You are the light of the world. A city set on a hill cannot be hidden."

MATTHEW 5:14

PRAY

Lord God, You have chosen me to be a light to the world. You place me so that I cannot be hidden from view in order that Your light will beam forth into the darkness. I pray that I will shine brighter today than yesterday. I will not hide myself away, but I will become a guiding light, bringing others directly to You! Thank You, Lord!

DECLARE

I am His light to the world. No more hiding! Let it shine!

He loves you so!

"And who would light a lamp and then hide it in an obscure place? Instead, it's placed where everyone in the house can benefit from its light."

MATTHEW 5:15 TPT

PRAY

Awesome God, reveal and uproot any place in me that is not living and thriving in Your truth. Shine Your glorious light on anything hidden in dark corners. Increase my capacity to shine brightly for You. May others notice Your light and ask why I am so hope-filled and joyful, so I can tell them about You. Thank You, Lord!

DECLARE

God's light shining through me is noticeable for all to see!

He loves you so!

"And if anyone forces you to go one mile, go with him two miles."

MATTHEW 5:41

PRAY

Abba Father, I pray that my whole life—all of my thoughts, words, actions, reactions, choices and relationships—be controlled by Christ's unconditional love living in me and through me. Help me to lean into You before I speak or act. May I walk in Your boldness and humility, continually offering grace and mercy to others. Thank You, Lord!

DECLARE

God's river of life and love flows through
me, drenching those around me!

He loves you so!

"But I say to you, Love your enemies and pray for those who persecute you."

MATTHEW 5:44

PRAY

Lord God, Your love is unconditional and all-encompassing, and that is the kind of love You want me to show others. In my own strength, that is often impossible. Please fill me and empower me, Holy Spirit, so that I can love everyone—family, friend or foe—in Your name, by Your strength and for Your glory. Thank You, Lord!

DECLARE

The Holy Spirit empowers me to love outside my own natural ability!

He loves you so!

"Whenever you pray, go into your innermost chamber and be alone with Father God, praying to him in secret. And your Father, who sees all you do, will reward you openly."

MATTHEW 6:6 TPT

PRAY

Father, today lead me to that place where You and I can meet . . . just the two of us. No one needs to know, and no one needs to hear. These times in the secret place help shape me into the person You created and called me to be. In that place, speak to me, sharing Your vision and birthing dreams. My heart yearns to join You there, to experience Your refreshing and to keep me focused on You. Thank You, Lord!

DECLARE

I yearn for and look forward to my time alone with God!

He loves you so!

"Do not be like them, for your Father knows what you need before you ask him."

MATTHEW 6:8

PRAY

Lord God, You are Jehovah-Jireh, my Provider. You know what all my needs will ever be. You know what I truly need far better than I even know. You are all-sufficient to provide for my every need. I lean on Your promise that You will never leave me lacking. Lord, please give me today what You know I need. Thank You, Lord!

DECLARE

God knows what I need better than I do!

He loves you so!

"Pray then like this: 'Our Father in heaven, hallowed be your name.'"

MATTHEW 6:9

PRAY

Abba Father, teach me to pray just as Jesus did with the disciples. Guide me to always begin by acknowledging who You are and where You dwell, to always show You the respect Your great name deserves. I am humbled that I can come boldly before Your throne to speak with You. I thank You for who You are and for all You have done. Thank You, Lord!

DECLARE

I can pray to my Father, who is in heaven,
and He hears me. Great is His name!

He loves you so!

"Your kingdom come, your will be done, on earth as it is in heaven."

MATTHEW 6:10

PRAY

Lord God, Your Kingdom has come. It is now. How I long to be Your conduit to flood this world with more of Your Presence and more worship of You in Spirit and truth. May I lead the way to make Your eternal Kingdom ways the priority in the Church, the culture, the world. Rain down, Lord! Thank You, Lord!

DECLARE

God's Kingdom has come—I close the gap between heaven and earth!

He loves you so!

"For where your treasure is, there your heart will be also."

MATTHEW 6:21

PRAY

Abba Lord, repeatedly Your Word says that those who seek You, find You. You want me to seek because it brings joy, excitement and adventure. And as I seek You, I am promised that I will find You. You are the greatest treasure of my life. I want You to assume Your rightful place of honor in my heart. Thank You, Lord!

DECLARE

God is my treasure, and that is where
my heart can be found!

He loves you so!

> "Therefore I tell you, do not be anxious about your life, what you will eat or what you will drink, nor about your body, what you will put on. Is not life more than food, and the body more than clothing?"

MATTHEW 6:25

PRAY

Almighty Lord, You and Your Kingdom are my first priority and my first assignment. There is nothing in this world that can even begin to compare with You. You have promised to meet all my needs according to Your riches in glory. You are always faithful to Your Word! Help me to trust You for my daily needs. You are my Provider. My hope is in You. Thank You, Lord!

DECLARE

I will not be anxious because my God
supplies all of my needs—every day!

He loves you so!

"But seek first the kingdom of God and his righteousness, and all these things will be added to you."

MATTHEW 6:33

PRAY

Almighty heavenly Father, teach me to continually seek Your Kingdom first and to follow after Your righteousness before I bring all my needs to You. I want to live in the miracle of watching You add all the things I need to my life. Thank You that I do not need to worry when I am trusting in and walking with You. Thank You, Lord!

DECLARE

Today I will seek His Kingdom and His righteousness first!

He loves you so!

"Refuse to be a critic full of bias toward others, and judgment will not be passed on you."

MATTHEW 7:1 TPT

PRAY

Gracious Lord, make me aware of the logs in my eyes that blur my vision. Please reveal and purge from me any form of hypocrisy that leads me to make wrong judgments of others. You have lavished grace on me, and I am not to keep it to myself. Help me to view others through Your eyes of love and grace. Thank You, Lord!

DECLARE

I am graced to be a grace giver!

He loves you so!

"Take my yoke upon you, and learn from me, for I am gentle and lowly in heart, and you will find rest for your souls."

MATTHEW 11:29

PRAY

King Jesus, striving and trying to do life my own way is tiresome and overly challenging. You break through all the chaos and discouragement of life and draw me close. In Your embrace my striving is replaced with surrender. My exhaustion is swallowed up by Your satisfying rest and peace. You alone are the rest my soul longs for! Thank You, Lord!

DECLARE

Exhaustion is overcome with rest
and peace in Jesus' Presence!

He loves you so!

"As for what was sown on good soil, this is the one who hears the word and understands it. He indeed bears fruit and yields, in one case a hundredfold, in another sixty, and in another thirty."

MATTHEW 13:23

PRAY

Lord of the harvest, I want to be Your good and fertile soil. Let my ears hear so that my spirit knows and understands Your perfect Word of Life. Sow Your seeds of light and truth in me so that they grow and produce a bountiful harvest. Your Word does not come back void, but it accomplishes abundantly more! Thank You, Lord!

DECLARE

I am good soil, producing a bountiful harvest!

He loves you so!

Simon Peter replied, "You are the Christ, the Son of the living God."

MATTHEW 16:16

PRAY

Precious Lord, thank You that the truth that You are the Christ—the Son of the Living God—is the firm foundation of Your Church. Father, bless the generations alive today with confidence and boldness to proclaim Your truth in love, to build Your Church and to encourage those who come after us, until You finally return. Thank You, Lord!

DECLARE

I stand firm on God's truth and
proclaim Jesus as Lord today!

He loves you so!

"Whoever humbles himself like this child is the greatest in the kingdom of heaven."

MATTHEW 18:4

PRAY

Abba Father, please help me to keep a humble and childlike heart. I want to brim with eagerness and excitement to grasp all that is just around the corner. I am ready and willing to keep in step with You, my kind Father. Help me keep in mind that I am not enough on my own. Please keep me humble and hungry so that I am ready to receive. Thank You, Lord!

DECLARE

Through the power of the Spirit, I stay humble and hungry, ready to receive more from God!

He loves you so!

And he said to him, "You shall love the Lord your God with all your heart and with all your soul and with all your mind."

MATTHEW 22:37

PRAY

King Jesus, even during times when I am being tested—like You were—You are working in me to know You more deeply. Knowing You more causes me to love You more. You are molding me and drawing me to love You with all my heart, all my soul and all my mind. Help me to go deeper into Your love today. Thank You, Lord!

DECLARE

I am growing in my knowledge of
God and loving Him more!

He loves you so!

A woman came up to him with an alabaster flask of very expensive ointment, and she poured it on his head as he reclined at table.

MATTHEW 26:7

PRAY

Almighty God, thank You that You get great joy and pleasure from extravagant worship. May I dance before You unrestrained, as a living sacrifice of praise. Help me to pour out my love to You with abandon, without fear or hesitation, even when others might think it foolish or wasteful. Help me not to worry or fear what others might think or how they might respond. Thank You, Lord!

DECLARE

I choose to worship with abandon and extravagance!

He loves you so!

"Go therefore and make disciples of all nations, baptizing them in the name of the Father and of the Son and of the Holy Spirit."

MATTHEW 28:19

PRAY

Abba Father, put Your love in my heart and Your words in my mouth that I may proclaim the Good News of Your grace to everyone I meet. Give me a passion for bringing others to You. Fill me with strength and wisdom so that I may be effective as a conduit of reconciling others to You. Thank You, Lord!

DECLARE

I am a living and active conduit of reconciliation!

He loves you so!

"Teaching them to observe all that I have commanded you. And behold, I am with you always, to the end of the age."

MATTHEW 28:20

PRAY

Lord God, thank You that You have assigned and commissioned me to teach others what You have taught me. You have anointed me to proclaim Your perfect truth. Help me to walk boldly in Your authority in my mission. I am equipped by Your Presence. Thank You that You walk with me each step of the way. Thank You, Lord!

DECLARE

I am walking daily in the commission
and anointing of King Jesus!

He loves you so!

And rising very early in the morning, while it was still dark, he departed and went out to a desolate place, and there he prayed.

MARK 1:35

PRAY

King Jesus, You are my example. You needed, wanted and desired to spend time alone with Abba Father. How much more do I need to make time alone with the Father a priority? I want to learn to talk with You throughout the day. I want to hear Your voice. Please alert me and help me recognize distractions that keep me from spending time alone with You. I know I need You. Thank You, Lord!

DECLARE

I have ears to hear the Great I Am's voice!

He loves you so!

When she heard about Jesus' healing power, she pushed through the crowd and came up from behind him and touched his prayer shawl.

MARK 5:27 TPT

PRAY

Father God, I know You have the power to heal all my sickness and pain. Empower me to press through all that would try to hinder me so that I can touch You. I push through all the chaos to be near You and be wrapped in Your Presence, where I am made whole. In You, I lack nothing. Thank You, Lord!

DECLARE

I will push through to the precious Presence of God!

He loves you so!

There was such a swirl of activity around Jesus, with so many people coming and going, that they were unable to even eat a meal. So Jesus said to his disciples, "Come, let's take a break and find a secluded place where you can rest a while."

MARK 6:31 TPT

PRAY

Sovereign Lord, You know that living in this world can be hard. It seems like there is so much to do and so little time to do it all. Lord, I want to take a break; I need a break. Take me away to our secluded place so I can invest time in Your Presence. Help me to quiet my concerns that I need to be part of all the activity, when really all I need is rest. Thank You, Lord!

DECLARE

Today I will enjoy resting with my King!

He loves you so!

And after he had taken leave of them, he went up on the mountain to pray.

MARK 6:46

PRAY

Holy Spirit, please nudge me and draw me to consistently step away from the daily craziness of life and get alone with You. Let my first and last thought every day be of You. Let my first and last words be Your name. Let my first and last actions be to kneel before You. Let my only impulse be to praise and worship You. Thank You, Lord!

DECLARE

Spending time with God is my lifeline and my joy!

He loves you so!

"For even the Son of Man came not to be served but to serve, and to give his life as a ransom for many."

MARK 10:45

PRAY

Sovereign Lord, invade my very being with Your passion, power and peace. Give me a heart like Jesus: a heart that is more ready to serve than to wait around to be served. A heart that is ready to get my hands dirty. A heart that is moved by Your compassion and willingness to help. A heart that is moved by what moves You. Thank You, Lord!

DECLARE

My heart is moved by what moves God!

He loves you so!

"Truly, I say to you, whoever says to this mountain, 'Be taken up and thrown into the sea,' and does not doubt in his heart, but believes that what he says will come to pass, it will be done for him."

MARK 11:23

PRAY

Almighty God, You parted the river and split the sea. You brought water from a rock. You calmed the storm and broke open prison doors. You made the way where there seemed to be no way. You are the Mountain Mover! You transform tragedy into triumph! You have always done it, and You will do it again. Thank You, Lord!

DECLARE

In Christ, I am a Mountain Mover, and therefore I declare the mountain to move, in Jesus' name!

He loves you so!

"The second is this: 'You shall love your neighbor as yourself.' There is no other commandment greater than these."

MARK 12:31

PRAY

Precious Lord, give me a heart to see my neighbor and to show mercy to others as You would. Position me and drive me to those who need Your touch of mercy to bring them some peace and healing. Lead me to stay on Your road and to love and serve all whom You lead into my path. Thank You, Lord!

DECLARE

I will be a neighbor, showing God's mercy,
no matter the inconvenience or cost!

He loves you so!

"Heaven and earth will pass away, but my words will not pass away."

MARK 13:31

PRAY

Father God, engrave Your Word on the very cells of my heart. Indelibly mark my being with You. Make Your Truth the wellspring of my life. Saturate every part of me so that Your love, Your promises, Your acceptance and Your delight soak into the very core of my being and become a fountain that floods my surroundings! Thank You, Lord!

DECLARE

God's Word saturates every corner of my heart and life!

He loves you so!

And he said to them, "As you go into all the world, preach openly the wonderful news of the gospel to the entire human race!"

MARK 16:15 TPT

PRAY

Lord God, stir up Your urgency within me to see the Gospel—the wonderful news about Jesus— reach every person. Give me a deeper vision and strategy to understand my "go" and the truth I should share. Build courage in me to say what You need me to say and to do what You tell me to do. Thank You, Lord!

DECLARE

I will go into my world and share the Gospel like wildfire!

He loves you so!

≣ For nothing will be impossible with God.

LUKE 1:37

PRAY

Unstoppable Lord, there is nothing that is too hard for You. Your perfect Word clearly reveals and declares not only what You can do, but who You are. You are the uncontainable, unlimited, all-powerful God. You are the nothing-is-impossible God! Let me live each moment in the reality of Your glorious truth that nothing is impossible for You. Thank You, Lord!

DECLARE

God cannot be stopped! My God is unstoppable!

He loves you so!

And she gave birth to her firstborn son and wrapped him in swaddling cloths and laid him in a manger, because there was no place for them in the inn.

LUKE 2:7

PRAY

Emmanuel, You are the God who is with us. I do not want to miss Your Presence today. Help me to make more room for You in my heart no matter what the day brings. Let there be nothing that crowds You out of my life. Bring intention to my life so there is always room for You. Thank You, Lord!

DECLARE

There is always room in my heart for more of Emmanuel—God with me!

He loves you so!

"For unto you is born this day in the city of David a Savior, who is Christ the Lord."

LUKE 2:11

PRAY

Abba Father, I celebrate and thank You that THE DAY came. THE DAY You had planned since the beginning of time. THE DAY prophets foretold. THE DAY when the Prince of Peace finally arrived. THE DAY Messiah invaded earth. THE DAY the Word became flesh to dwell with me. In HIM all Your promises are Yes and Amen! Thank You, Lord!

DECLARE

I receive God's promises of YES and AMEN!

He loves you so!

John answered them all, saying, "I baptize you with water, but he who is mightier than I is coming, the strap of whose sandals I am not worthy to untie. He will baptize you with the Holy Spirit and fire."

LUKE 3:16

PRAY

Holy Spirit, come and ignite my heart with Your holy fire. Set my life ablaze with the fire of Your Presence. I pray that my every breath burns brightly for You as I passionately pursue more of You. May Your Presence in me spark wildfires in others as Your Kingdom invades this world. You are worth it all. Thank You, Lord!

DECLARE

The Holy Spirit burns brightly and
passionately in and through me!

He loves you so!

"The Spirit of the Lord is upon me, and he has anointed me to be hope for the poor, freedom for the brokenhearted, and new eyes for the blind, and to preach to prisoners, 'You are set free!'"

LUKE 4:18 TPT

PRAY

Father, I pray that as Your vessel, I will be an answer to someone's prayer. Use me to bring Your Good News to all who need to hear it, Your freedom to the oppressed, Your restoration and miracles to the hurting and Your healing to the sick, in Jesus' name. Let me get out of the way so that You can work through me to change lives! Thank You, Lord!

DECLARE

The Good News of Jesus flows through my veins!

He loves you so!

He began by saying to them, "Today this scripture is fulfilled in your hearing."

LUKE 4:21 NIV

PRAY

King Jesus, engrave Your truth on my mind and my heart. You have called me to continue the work that You started and to do even greater things. Free me from any attitudes, lies or stubbornness that would keep me from living in Your plan to the fullest. Help me to live confidently, led by Your example and bold in the anointing that You have poured out on me. Thank You, Lord!

DECLARE

I will live a life that fulfills all that God
has written about my life!

He loves you so!

"Be merciful, even as your Father is merciful."

LUKE 6:36

PRAY

Lord, thank You for always being generous in Your mercy and forgiveness. Your mercy gives me what I could never earn on my own. Help me to show that same mercy to others. Whenever my first response is to lash out, stop me in my tracks and help me to remember the mercy You have shown to me. Help me to be Your instrument of mercy in the lives of others. Thank You, Lord!

DECLARE

I am God's instrument of generous mercy today!

He loves you so!

In that same hour he rejoiced in the Holy Spirit and said, "I thank you, Father, Lord of heaven and earth, that you have hidden these things from the wise and understanding and revealed them to little children; yes, Father, for such was your gracious will."

LUKE 10:21

PRAY

Abba Father, in Your gracious plan You choose to work through ordinary people. You choose to reveal Your purpose to the ordinary. Ordinary people who believe and know that You are Extraordinary. Ordinary people who believe that You turn the world upside down in and through them. Ordinary people are Your extraordinary conduit to deliver Your love and bring You glory. Thank You, Lord!

DECLARE

My ordinary is transformed into God's conduit of His extraordinary revelations!

He loves you so!

And he answered, "You shall love the Lord your God with all your heart and with all your soul and with all your strength and with all your mind, and your neighbor as yourself."

LUKE 10:27

PRAY

Lord and Master, You gave us the greatest commandment of all: to love God with all that I am—heart, soul, strength and mind. I do not want to be flippant when I say to You, "I love You." I do not ever want to take Your love casually. I want my life to be characterized by loving You with all that is within me! Thank You, Lord!

DECLARE

My love for Almighty God encompasses
all of me and overflows to others!

He loves you so!

"Simply be confident and allow the Spirit of Wisdom access to your heart, and he will reveal in that very moment what you are to say to them."

LUKE 12:12 TPT

PRAY

Abba Father, I want to know You so intimately that Your response is my first reaction. You have complete entry to my whole heart. Speak through me to release Your words of encouragement and Your heart of love to those who need to hear from You. Use me, by the power of the Holy Spirit, to glorify You in all I say and do. Thank You, Lord!

DECLARE

I am confident that the Spirit will give me the right words to say when they are needed!

He loves you so!

"What man of you, having a hundred sheep, if he has lost one of them, does not leave the ninety-nine in the open country, and go after the one that is lost, until he finds it?"

LUKE 15:4

PRAY

My Good Shepherd, You left heaven, everything You knew, to seek after me. I am the lost one You went after. I am the great treasure that You patiently sought after. Thank You for continuing to search until I was found! Help me to follow Your example, to leave things behind to seek after the one. Thank You, Lord!

DECLARE

Like the Good Shepherd, I stop for the one!

He loves you so!

"No servant can serve two masters, for either he will hate the one and love the other, or he will be devoted to the one and despise the other. You cannot serve God and money."

LUKE 16:13

PRAY

Lord God, You alone are my true Lord and Master. Help me to be devoted to You and to serve You alone with all my heart, soul, mind and strength. A divided heart cannot survive in me. I desire Your righteousness, Your faithfulness, Your will and Your way to rule my life. Lead me to faithfully and wisely walk in step with You. Thank You, Lord!

DECLARE

God is my one and only true need and desire!

He loves you so!

Then one of them, when he saw that he was healed, turned back, praising God with a loud voice.

LUKE 17:15

PRAY

Father God, You are always working and always moving. You never rest or take a day off. May I recognize Your work in and around me. May I daily realize: "Wow! I prayed for this! Here it is! It is happening!" Your answer is now. I want to seize every opportunity to come back praising and glorifying You with a loud voice. Thank You, Lord!

DECLARE

God is working in and through my life right now! Today!

He loves you so!

He answered, "I tell you, if these were silent, the very stones would cry out."

LUKE 19:40

PRAY

Abba Father, as long as I have voice, no stones will cry out. You are the Almighty Creator. I am Your very good creation. You are the One and Only Savior. I am saved. You are the Deliverer. I am delivered. You are the Healer. I am healed. You are the Restorer. I am restored. You are the Redeemer. I am redeemed. You are the All-Consuming Fire. I am consumed with and by You. Thank You, Lord!

DECLARE

I will shout my praise to God, holding nothing back!

He loves you so!

The women were terrified and bowed their faces to the ground, but the men said to them, "Why do you search for the living among the dead? He is not here, but He is risen!"

LUKE 24:5–6 TLV

PRAY

King Jesus, You conquered death! You overcame the grave! The tomb was found empty, and it stays that way today. You rose, just as You promised! You are alive! You are seated on Your throne! You reign in victory! The ultimate price has been paid! The perfect way has been made! The greatest victory has been won! Jesus is alive! Thank You, Lord!

DECLARE

My God is not dead! He is alive and active today!

He loves you so!

The light shines in the darkness, and the darkness has not overcome it.

JOHN 1:5

PRAY

Holy Spirit, Your Light is too brilliant and glorious to be overshadowed or extinguished. Your Light breaks through the darkest night. I will not live my life quietly hidden away, hiding Your Light. My life and my goal is to make Your brilliance conspicuous. I was called to be Your Light, shining bright, using it to break through darkness with Your overcoming truth. Thank You, Lord!

DECLARE

I was created to be a conspicuous light shining in the dark!

He loves you so!

The Word became flesh and made his dwelling among us. We have seen his glory, the glory of the one and only Son, who came from the Father, full of grace and truth.

JOHN 1:14 NIV

PRAY

Precious Lord, how I pray that I would cease striving after what You have freely given. I pray to live in the reality that You want to be with me and that You enjoy my presence even more than I enjoy Your Presence. I am so grateful You came to dwell with me—each and every day. Thank You, Lord!

DECLARE

God loves me so much that He has made His dwelling with me!

He loves you so!

The next day he saw Jesus coming toward him, and said, "Behold, the Lamb of God, who takes away the sin of the world!"

JOHN 1:29

PRAY

King Jesus, You knew where and when I was wandering alone, completely lost. But You came to me as the perfect sacrifice, the Lamb slain before the foundation of the earth. You have accomplished what I could never do on my own. Your blood washed my sins away. Thank You for Your mercy, forgiveness, redemption, restoration and love. Thank You, Lord!

DECLARE

The Lamb of God sacrificed His life for me!

He loves you so!

"And now I have seen with discernment. I can tell you for sure that this man is the Son of God."

JOHN 1:34 TPT

PRAY

Creator, for this moment in time, You have molded me as a witness that You alone are the One and Only True, Living God. Thank You for allowing me to be an eyewitness of Your excellence. You work and move in and through my life as evidence to me and to those around me that You are here now. Thank You, Lord!

DECLARE

"Immanuel" is my "with me" God—always and forever!

He loves you so!

"Come, see a man who told me all that I ever did. Can this be the Christ?"

JOHN 4:29

PRAY

Precious Jesus, open my eyes to see You in the interruptions of my life, in each of those divine-appointment moments. Help me to slow down and seize each of those moments. Guide me to take the time from whatever I have scheduled to receive Your special treasures of love and grace. Embolden me to invite others to come and see You too. Thank You, Lord!

DECLARE

I seize and treasure God-interruptions in my day!

He loves you so!

Jesus answered his critics by saying, "Every day my Father is at work, and I will be too!"

JOHN 5:17 TPT

PRAY

Almighty, Everlasting God, You are always loving, working, moving and happening. You are Right Now! You are not just the God who was or even the God who will be one day. You are the God of the present! You are currently happening! You are the God of today! You are the God of this moment! Hallelujah! Thank You, Lord!

DECLARE

God is at work in me at this very moment!

He loves you so!

"So if the Son sets you free, you will be free indeed."

JOHN 8:36

PRAY

Lord, thank You for defeating sin and death and for paving the way for me to enjoy freedom in You. I am no longer tied up and held captive. I am free indeed! Teach me to live out my freedom as I worship You, when I pray and as I go about my day. Father, forgive me whenever I take my precious freedom for granted. Thank You, Lord!

DECLARE

The Son has set me free; therefore, I am free indeed!

He loves you so!

"The thief comes only to steal and kill and destroy. I came that they may have life and have it abundantly."

JOHN 10:10

PRAY

Lord God, guard the path that I walk from the enemy, who wants only to steal, kill and destroy my relationship with You. May Your perfect plans never be thwarted; they can never be. Help me to live in the abundant life You provided through Your Son, Jesus. Enable and equip me to overthrow the plans of the thief. Thank You, Lord!

DECLARE

Abundant life is God's perfect promise to me!

He loves you so!

"My sheep hear my voice, and I know them, and they follow me."

JOHN 10:27

PRAY

Precious Lord, when I cry out to You, You hear me. You know the sound of my voice, and You answer me. You already know what I am going to be facing and what I am going to need. You go before me, You go after me, You go each step with me. You surround me. You are always with me. Thank You, Lord!

DECLARE

God knows the sound of my voice,
and I know the sound of His!

He loves you so!

"If I then, your Lord and Teacher, have washed your feet, you also ought to wash one another's feet."

JOHN 13:14

PRAY

Jesus, Rabboni, as always, You are the perfect example of a teacher and servant-leader. You would not ask me to do something that You Yourself would not do. As I go out as Your hands and voice to those around me, give me Your attitude of a humble servant. Help me to love and serve selflessly, like You did. Thank You, Lord!

DECLARE

I am the hands and voice of God to the world today!

He loves you so!

"By this all people will know that you are my disciples, if you have love for one another."

JOHN 13:35

PRAY

Abba Father, I want to be known as Yours. Help my eyes to see where love is needed—even if it is in the most difficult circumstances. Please love others through me, as Your perfect love can kick down all their walls. May I be Your love in word and action so others can step into their God-given identities. Thank You, Lord!

DECLARE

Because I am greatly loved and known as His, I love generously!

He loves you so!

"And if I go and prepare a place for you, I will come again and will take you to myself, that where I am you may be also."

JOHN 14:3

PRAY

Almighty God, what a wonderful thought, that You, the Creator of all heaven and earth, will one day welcome me home. One day I will stand before You, in the very Presence of the One I have longed to see. You desire to have me home, where You are. Thank You for Your marvelous promise that You are preparing a place for me in heaven. Thank You, Lord!

DECLARE

Even before I am in heaven, I am accepted and welcomed into God's Presence!

He loves you so!

"If you had known me, you would have known my Father also. From now on you do know him and have seen him."

JOHN 14:7

PRAY

Abba Father, thank You that every word and work of Jesus reveals who You are to me. Jesus redeems and reveals You as Redeemer. Jesus heals and reveals You as Healer. Jesus delivers and reveals You as Deliverer. Jesus provides and reveals You as Provider. Jesus reveals that You are compassionate, kind, all-powerful and so much more. Thank You, Lord!

DECLARE

Jesus reveals God to me so that I can reveal His love, mercy and great goodness to others!

He loves you so!

"Truly, truly, I say to you, whoever believes in me will also do the works that I do; and greater works than these will he do, because I am going to the Father."

JOHN 14:12

PRAY

King Jesus, You gave sight to the blind. You made the lame walk. You opened deaf ears. You raised the dead. You fed multitudes. You walked on water. Please release hope to my discouraged heart. Come and calm my storms. You accept this outcast, and You love with an everlasting love. Help me to do these things, as well as the "greater works" You ask of me. Holy Spirit, make me an effective conduit of God's miracle power to others. Thank You, Lord!

DECLARE

I follow in Jesus' footsteps—releasing His Presence and power everywhere I go!

He loves you so!

"Even the Spirit of truth, whom the world cannot receive, because it neither sees him nor knows him. You know him, for he dwells with you and will be in you."

JOHN 14:17

PRAY

Holy Spirit, the world has no hold on me because You are God living in and through me. I want to know You more. Please help me to grow closer to You. Take me deeper in Your truth and give me an understanding of who You are. I long to know so much more as I walk daily with You. Thank You, Lord!

DECLARE

God's Presence living in and through me has a name—the Holy Spirit!

He loves you so!

"But the Helper, the Holy Spirit, whom the Father will send in my name, he will teach you all things and bring to your remembrance all that I have said to you."

JOHN 14:26

PRAY

Lord, because of the Holy Spirit, I am equipped and strengthened to know Your ways. I can always see when, where and how You are moving. As soon as my eyes see or my ears hear, help me to respond instantly to You. I want to be ready to take risks and bring Your Presence wherever You lead me. Thank You, Lord!

DECLARE

The Holy Spirit teaches, instructs, equips and guides me!

He loves you so!

"Peace I leave with you; my peace I give to you. Not as the world gives do I give to you. Let not your hearts be troubled, neither let them be afraid."

JOHN 14:27

PRAY

Almighty Lord, I need Your perfect peace. The world's version of peace is incomplete and temporary at best. When I rely on that false peace, whenever something bad happens, true peace slips from my grasp. But the peace You give lives inside me. It carries me far beyond my expectations. Your genuine peace overflows in and through me. Thank You, Lord!

DECLARE

I have the peace that passes my human understanding!

He loves you so!

"I am the vine; you are the branches. Whoever abides in me and I in him, he it is that bears much fruit, for apart from me you can do nothing."

JOHN 15:5

PRAY

Lord God, the True Vine, do not let me waste a single day, not a single moment, that could be used to grow deeper in love and in my relationship with You. I want to know You more and release Your Presence faithfully with all that I am and all that I have. Help me to show others who You are. Thank You, Lord!

DECLARE

I am a living branch of the True Vine,
bearing fruit for the Kingdom!

He loves you so!

Greater love has no one than this, that someone lay down his life for his friends.

JOHN 15:13

PRAY

Father God, I know that You understand that freedom is not free. My spiritual freedom cost You the life of Your only Son. Jesus obediently and willingly gave His life for me. He paid the ultimate price in my place. May I boldly build on Jesus' obedience and sacrifice to secure and release true freedom for many more today and for future generations. Thank You, Lord!

DECLARE

Jesus was faithful to demonstrate greater love,
and I choose to follow His example!

He loves you so!

"I have never called you 'servants,' because a master doesn't confide in his servants, and servants don't always understand what the master is doing. But I call you my most intimate friends, for I reveal to you everything that I've heard from my Father."

JOHN 15:15 TPT

PRAY

King Jesus, You have drawn me close and made the way for me to be Your friend. You do not stand at a distance. You do not keep me at arm's length. You welcome me into Your presence. You are personal and intimate in my life. May my life vividly display that You are the Holy One of God! Thank You, Lord!

DECLARE

I can lay my head against God's chest
and hear Jesus' heartbeat!

He loves you so!

"You did not choose me, but I chose you and appointed you that you should go and bear fruit and that your fruit should abide, so that whatever you ask the Father in my name, he may give it to you."

JOHN 15:16

PRAY

Abba Daddy, remind me deep down in the very core of my soul that You chose me. You wanted me, so You created me! You formed me, and You made me Your child! I am wanted! I am welcomed! I am cherished! I am loved! I am anointed! I am called! You appointed me and have made me worthy! Thank You, Lord!

DECLARE

I am chosen by Adonai—the Lord and Master of all—to abide in Him and bear much fruit!

He loves you so!

"But here's the truth: It's to your advantage that I go away, for if I don't go away the Divine Encourager will not be released to you. But after I depart, I will send him to you."

JOHN 16:7 TPT

PRAY

King Jesus, You sent Your Holy Spirit as my encouragement, comfort and holy envoy. He is my advantage, reminding me daily of Your will and Your way. He is my help, giving me the ability to follow in Your footsteps. He is a glorious Person and Your empowering Presence on me and in me and through my life. Thank You, Lord!

DECLARE

Jesus' Presence in the world today has a name—the Holy Spirit!

He loves you so!

"When the Spirit of truth comes, he will guide you into all the truth, for he will not speak on his own authority, but whatever he hears he will speak, and he will declare to you the things that are to come."

JOHN 16:13

PRAY

Holy Spirit, saturate every part of my being! Consume me with Your Presence. I am Your house, Your dwelling place, Your current tabernacle in the world. Overflow through my life boldly and vibrantly as I learn to carry Your Presence every day, in every way, everywhere. It is in You that I live and move and have my being. Thank You, Lord!

DECLARE

The Holy Spirit tabernacles in me and moves through me!

He loves you so!

"I have said these things to you, that in me you may have peace. In the world you will have tribulation. But take heart; I have overcome the world."

JOHN 16:33

PRAY

Lord God, You have overcome and conquered everything that I will ever encounter in this world. You empower me with strength. You equip me with courage. You are my Source to boldly step forward in Your truth. Even in times of trouble and sorrow, I can stand firm in perfect peace because You are the Unshakeable God! Thank You, Lord!

DECLARE

The Peace living in me has conquered the world!

He loves you so!

≡ Sanctify them in the truth; your word is truth.

JOHN 17:17

PRAY

Lord God, move my heart to savor and delight in Your truth. Give me a hunger to read, study and memorize the Word that You have provided at such a cost. It is Your precious love letter to me. I want to have it written on my heart. Let it do Your work to set me apart as Yours. Give me the understanding to apply it to every area of my life. Thank You, Lord!

DECLARE

God's Word is truth, and it sets me apart!

He loves you so!

"As you sent me into the world, so I have sent them into the world."

JOHN 17:18

PRAY

Abba Father, thank You for the territory—the sphere of influence—in which You have placed and positioned me. Help me to connect and build relationships and cause me to truly listen in conversations that build bridges to You. May Your love overflow through me so that I can love with Your love, so that others see You and know You. Thank You, Lord!

DECLARE

God's divine connection flows through me
to influence the world around me!

He loves you so!

On the evening of that day, the first day of the week, the doors being locked where the disciples were for fear of the Jews, Jesus came and stood among them and said to them, "Peace be with you."

JOHN 20:19

PRAY

All-seeing Lord, open my eyes to recognize Your Presence that is here now. May I constantly be watching for You and Your movement. Even if it does not make sense to me or is very different from what I would expect, I want to continually see You. You are always working and moving. Help me to see You. Thank You, Lord!

DECLARE

God is here now and has given me eyes to see Him!

He loves you so!

And divided tongues as of fire appeared to them and rested on each one of them.

ACTS 2:3

PRAY

Precious Messiah and Savior, thank You for sending the promised Holy Spirit. I want to walk fully in the Holy Spirit's power and guidance. Help me to live in such a way that the Holy Spirit is released from my box of limitations. Make Him vivid and apparent in and through me so that He is more visible to all. Thank You, Lord!

DECLARE

I am a dwelling place of the Holy Spirit. His empowering Presence is on, in and through me!

He loves you so!

Now when they saw the boldness of Peter and John, and perceived that they were uneducated, common men, they were astonished. And they recognized that they had been with Jesus.

ACTS 4:13

PRAY

Sovereign God, Your unmatched power was displayed through ordinary people who became extraordinary disciples and leaders. Because of Jesus, that same power and strength that worked through them now lives and works through me. Through Jesus' blood, my ordinary life displays my extraordinary Lord. Help me to live my life openly so that others recognize the difference in me, which is You. Thank You, Lord!

DECLARE

God has called me to be extraordinarily ordinary so that I can reveal Jesus!

He loves you so!

"It's impossible for us to stop speaking about all the things we've seen and heard!"

ACTS 4:20 TPT

PRAY

Lord God, all that You do is beyond definition. You have asked me to talk about You, but honestly, at times, I cannot find the words to accurately tell others about You. You are too good for mere human words. Give me Your words! I pray for a fresh touch on my words to declare Your amazing ways with fresh boldness. Thank You, Lord!

DECLARE

I am compelled to declare the amazing works of God! I must proclaim His greatness!

He loves you so!

And when they had prayed, the place in which they were gathered together was shaken, and they were all filled with the Holy Spirit and continued to speak the word of God with boldness.

ACTS 4:31

PRAY

Glorious King Jesus, I pray to live a radical life empowered by Your Holy Spirit. I have experienced You working through me, and I am hungry for more. I long to be Your vessel, speaking Your words of life with holy boldness. As You have done it before, I ask, in Jesus' name, please do it again! Thank You, Lord!

DECLARE

I am filled with God's Spirit, and I
speak His Word with boldness!

He loves you so!

And when they could not find them, they dragged Jason and some of the brothers before the city authorities, shouting, "These men who have turned the world upside down have come here also."

ACTS 17:6

PRAY

Abba Father, my heart knows that the status quo of this world is no longer acceptable. Help me to live before others in such a way that Your will and Your ways are seen as the desired norm. May there be enough evidence in my life that I am counted as one who has turned the world upside down with Your mercy, grace and love. Thank You, Lord!

DECLARE

My faith and my life turn the world upside down!

He loves you so!

"For 'In him we live and move and have our being'; as even some of your own poets have said, 'For we are indeed his offspring.'"

ACTS 17:28

PRAY

Lord, You permeate my entire being. You cause me to truly live and move and be who You created me to be. As Your child, help me to comprehend that You are not just a part of my day, but that You are the point of my day. I want to live and move in what You are doing today and be a part of it! Thank You, Lord!

DECLARE

As a child of God, it is in Christ that I live and move and find my purpose!

He loves you so!

Epistles

For I long to see you, so I may share with you some spiritual gift to strengthen you.

ROMANS 1:11 TLV

PRAY

Abba Father, You have abundantly blessed me and created me to be a blessing. You made me to be Your blessing to Your children. I pray that my self-made walls crumble and fall so that You can work in and through me to spiritually encourage, build up and strengthen my brothers and sisters in You and for You. Thank You, Lord!

DECLARE

God created me to be a beautiful
blessing to the body of Christ!

He loves you so!

They exchanged the truth about God for a lie and worshiped and served the creature rather than the Creator, who is blessed forever! Amen.

ROMANS 1:25

PRAY

Lord of lords, You have lavished me with blessing after blessing. Hinder me from worshiping Your blessings over You. Help me to serve You, the Creator, with my whole heart. Embolden me to hold on to the truth and reject the lies the world tells about You. Remind me to gird my mind with Your Word so that I may carefully walk in Your ways. Thank You, Lord!

DECLARE

God is the One I worship. He is most blessed forever!

He loves you so!

You also must consider yourselves dead to sin and alive to God in Christ Jesus.

ROMANS 6:11

PRAY

Redeeming Lord, there are moments when the mess and chaos of my past come flooding back in my mind, not to mention the regret of current wrong choices. Please forgive me for recalling what You have already forgiven. Help me be quick to ask for forgiveness of present issues. Lord, remind me that because of You, I am dead to sin but alive in You. Thank You, Lord!

DECLARE

Sin no longer has a hold on me because I am alive in Christ!

He loves you so!

So now the case is closed. There remains no accusing voice of condemnation against those who are joined in life-union with Jesus, the Anointed One.

ROMANS 8:1 TPT

PRAY

Father God, the Righteous Judge, You declared the case against me closed. Any voice of regret, doubt or condemnation is not from You. Those thoughts are from the accuser. Help me to re-mind the enemy that Jesus paid the penalty for all my sin. Enable me to live unapologetically in Your forgiveness, mercy, grace and love. Thank You, Lord!

DECLARE

The true and just verdict is that I am free! Case closed!

He loves you so!

For I consider that the sufferings of this present time are not worth comparing with the glory that is to be revealed to us.

ROMANS 8:18

PRAY

Sovereign Lord, no matter the chaos around me, You are always in control. Build my faith to believe that anything I might face pales in comparison to the glory that is being revealed to me through the situation. Remind me that You are Lord of my past, my present and my future. You are working all things together for my good. Thank You, Lord!

DECLARE

God's glory and majesty far outshine anything I face!

He loves you so!

We know that for those who love God all things work together for good, for those who are called according to his purpose.

ROMANS 8:28

PRAY

Sovereign God, You alone provide the assurance I need. You are always in control. You are the authority that ensures that nothing can touch me without Your permission. I thank You for working out Your purpose, even through the difficult circumstances of my life. If something does reach me, I can rest in the promise that You are already working it out. Thank You, Lord!

DECLARE

God is always working and orchestrating circumstances for my good!

He loves you so!

He who did not spare his own Son but gave him up for us all, how will he not also with him graciously give us all things?

ROMANS 8:32

PRAY

Lord God, out of the fullness of Christ Jesus, You have blessed me with everything I will ever need. You will never withhold anything good from me. Because You are never stingy or miserly, I can draw from the well of Your abundant and boundless provision for my every sin, my every failure and my every need. Thank You, Lord!

DECLARE

God will graciously give me all the things I need!

He loves you so!

Who shall bring any charge against God's elect? It is God who justifies.

ROMANS 8:33

PRAY

Almighty Lord, I thank You and praise You for giving me a new life in Christ. The old me is gone. You have made me new. When the enemy comes at me with accusations, thank You that my past no longer has a hold on me! Help me to reject the lies of the enemy and to live my life justified by Your truth. Thank You, Lord!

DECLARE

My past has been expunged, and I live in God's approval!

He loves you so!

Nor height nor depth, nor anything else in all creation, will be able to separate us from the love of God in Christ Jesus our Lord.

ROMANS 8:39

PRAY

Christ, my Lord, when the enemy whispers in my ear that You do not love me, please draw me close. When I feel discouraged, let Your love lead me to Your truth. When I am feeling defeated by my own weaknesses and failures, wrap Your arms of unfailing love around me. Let the Holy Spirit continually bring to mind that there is not one thing that can ever separate us. Thank You, Lord!

DECLARE

There is nothing that can separate me from God's love!

He loves you so!

For the Scripture says, "Everyone who believes in him will not be put to shame."

ROMANS 10:11

PRAY

Awesome Lord, Your faithfulness is wonderful and amazing! You did not create me to live in shame because shame has never been in Your plan. In You all shame is destroyed. Thank You for providing the ultimate defense against this scheme of the enemy and thwarting his plans against me. I believe in You, and shame has no place in me! Thank You, Lord!

DECLARE

Shame no longer has a hold on me; I belong to the Shame Breaker!

He loves you so!

And how are they to preach unless they are sent? As it is written, "How beautiful are the feet of those who preach the good news!"

ROMANS 10:15

PRAY

Almighty God of all nations, tribes and tongues, cause my heart to hurt like Yours to see so many people in the world without knowledge of You and Your Good News. Holy Spirit, stir me to go where I am sent; to be the beautiful feet of Jesus and deliver the Good News so that people have the opportunity to be added to Your Kingdom. Thank You, Lord!

DECLARE

I am a sent one, on a mission to share God's Good News!

He loves you so!

So faith comes from hearing, and hearing through the word of Christ.

ROMANS 10:17

PRAY

Lord, thank You for Your Word. Thank You for the power it contains. Thank You for the truths it reveals. Thank You for the peace it provides. Thank You for the joy it ignites. Thank You for the faith that it grows. Thank You that I am equipped through Your Word and that it strengthens me for Your work. Thank You, Lord!

DECLARE

I am attentive to God's Word of truth!

He loves you so!

When God chooses someone and graciously imparts gifts to him, they are never rescinded.

ROMANS 11:29 TPT

PRAY

Almighty God, not only have You chosen me, but You have also graciously gifted me with all I need. Help me to effectively wield the gifts You have placed within me so that I may live out my days as You have written them in Your book. Help me to never waste what You have given and to see those gifts increase with good use. Thank You, Lord!

DECLARE

God has given me gifts that will glorify Him!

He loves you so!

Love does no wrong to a neighbor; therefore love is the fulfilling of the law.

ROMANS 13:10

PRAY

Lord God, whenever someone wounds me or insults me, my first reaction is to lash out, right back at them. I know You have a better way—the way of love. Help me to respond in love instead of reacting in kind. Help me not to dwell on my "rights," but on what is right in Your eyes. Thank You, Lord!

DECLARE

I choose to walk in God's love, even
in the face of hurt and pain!

He loves you so!

For whatever was written in former days was written for our instruction, that through endurance and through the encouragement of the Scriptures we might have hope.

ROMANS 15:4

PRAY

Holy Lord, Your precious Word holds the key to receive hope. Please strengthen me to continue pushing through so that I discover that key as the treasure of my life when I read Your Word. Birth Your true hope in me. Help me to echo Your Word of hope in my own heart and to others around me. Thank You, Lord!

DECLARE

Jesus—the Way, the Truth and the Life—
the Living Word—echoes through me!

He loves you so!

Now may God, the inspiration and fountain of hope, fill you to overflowing with uncontainable joy and perfect peace as you trust in him. And may the power of the Holy Spirit continually surround your life with his super-abundance until you radiate with hope!

ROMANS 15:13 TPT

PRAY

Almighty God, the Fountain of Hope, You repeatedly lavish my life with Your uncontainable joy and peace. Your peace drenches and overflows everything that concerns me. You strengthen me and infuse me with joy, courage and strength through the Holy Spirit. May Your hope, joy and peace be the gold thread woven into the dailiness of my life. Thank You, Lord!

DECLARE

The dailiness of my life is woven together
with God's hope, joy and peace!

He loves you so!

But God chose what is foolish in the world to shame the wise; God chose what is weak in the world to shame the strong.

1 CORINTHIANS 1:27

PRAY

Loving Lord, I am not the strongest or the wisest, so I thank You that I have been chosen just as I am. You replace my weakness with Your abundant strength. Please lead me to draw upon that strength and help me to live a life that glorifies You. Remind me that I never have to go it alone. Thank You, Lord!

DECLARE

God chose me, even with my weaknesses,
to show how strong and mighty He is!

He loves you so!

My speech and my message were not in plausible words of wisdom, but in demonstration of the Spirit and of power.

1 CORINTHIANS 2:4

PRAY

Holy Spirit, I pray to be Your lightning rod to bring Your Good News to others. But I do not want to be a person who merely argues and debates. I pray that Your power and love are so evident that people actually see how amazing and real You are. Use me any time to release the reality of Your power and Your Kingdom! Thank You, Lord!

DECLARE

I am a lightning rod of God's Presence and power!

He loves you so!

So that your faith might not rest in the wisdom of men but in the power of God.

1 CORINTHIANS 2:5

PRAY

All-knowing Lord, thank You for the effective words of the wise teachers You have positioned and placed in my path. You helped me to learn from them, but more than that, You make me confident and bold through the demonstration of Your Spirit's power. May it be so! Let my faith rest solely in Your amazing power. Thank You, Lord!

DECLARE

My faith is firmly rooted and growing
in the power of the Holy Spirit!

He loves you so!

What no eye has seen, nor ear heard, nor the heart of man imagined, what God has prepared for those who love him.

1 CORINTHIANS 2:9

PRAY

Father God, what You have prepared for me makes my heart resound with praise. You have so much more in store for me than I can imagine. Don't let that limit You! I declare that You are doing a new thing that is beginning right now. I anticipate Your something new, something never seen before. Give me Your wisdom to know it when I see it and to respond in obedience. Thank You, Lord!

DECLARE

God's new things are happening in and through me now!

He loves you so!

We are coworkers with God and you are God's cultivated garden, the house he is building.

1 CORINTHIANS 3:9 TPT

PRAY

Precious Lord, I am in awe and wonder that You would call me Your partner, Your co-worker. That is what I am! I am Your rich and fruitful field, the house You are constructing. As You build me, help me to remember and cling to Your endless wisdom, Your limitless power and Your unending love. It is Your Holy Spirit that equips and empowers me. Thank You, Lord!

DECLARE

I am God's co-worker, being built by Him!

He loves you so!

Don't you realize that together you have become God's inner sanctuary and that the Spirit of God makes his permanent home in you?

1 CORINTHIANS 3:16 TPT

PRAY

Yahweh Lord, fully inhabit my body, soul, mind and spirit. Move me. Speak to me. Speak through me. It is almost too much to comprehend that I am the dwelling place for You, Almighty God. You have made me Your permanent home, Your earthly dwelling place, and I have the privilege of carrying Your Presence wherever I go. Thank You, Lord!

DECLARE

I am the living, breathing, moving dwelling place of God!

He loves you so!

This is how one should regard us, as servants of Christ and stewards of the mysteries of God.

1 CORINTHIANS 4:1

PRAY

Lord, my heart's desire is that when someone thinks of me, they think I am Your servant. I often fall short of that descriptor, so please help me to reach higher. You have entrusted me as a steward of the mysteries surrounding You, especially the greatest mystery: Christ in me, the hope of glory. Give me eyes to see whom You want me to serve and share the mystery with. May all my conversations and relationships honor You. Thank You, Lord!

DECLARE

I am God's servant, and my words and actions steward the mysteries of Yahweh!

He loves you so!

≡ So I do not run aimlessly; I do not box as one beating the air.

1 Corinthians 9:26

PRAY

Holy Spirit, help me not to go through life flailing around with no purpose or intention. I do not want to expend energy that does not produce potency. With purpose and effectiveness is the way I run the race before me. You enable me to run my race with intent in such a way as to receive the prize. Thank You, Lord!

DECLARE

I will run my race with purpose and intent!

He loves you so!

I train like a champion athlete. I subdue my body and get it under my control, so that after preaching the good news to others I myself won't be disqualified.

1 CORINTHIANS 9:27 TPT

PRAY

Father God, I want my life to count for Your eternal purposes. Do not let me lose my value to Your Kingdom purposes by compromising my standards or seeking friendships with the world. I do not want my life to be void. Help my every choice to be made with Your Kingdom and eternal values in focus. Thank You, Lord!

DECLARE

My life will not be disqualified. God is making me His champion!

He loves you so!

Remember, it is the same Holy Spirit who distributes, activates, and operates these different gifts as he chooses for each believer.

1 CORINTHIANS 12:11 TPT

PRAY

Holy Spirit, You are alive and active in me to accomplish the impossible. Without Your Presence living in me, there is no way that I could live, move or have my being. You have given to me and activated amazing gifts in my life. Please do the impossible even more in and through me. It is my great joy to be Your vessel. Thank You, Lord!

DECLARE

I am activated by the Spirit and operating
in the gifts He has given me!

He loves you so!

For the body does not consist of one member but of many.

1 CORINTHIANS 12:14

PRAY

Lord, thank You for the gifts You have given and equipped me with. I admit, though, sometimes I wonder what kind of difference just little ol' me can possibly make. You have given me this moment in time. Lead me in using Your gifts for Your glory and for the good of all Your children. Speak to my heart, I pray, and show me how You want to work through me today. Thank You, Lord!

DECLARE

God purposed me to release His Presence during this time in HIStory!

He loves you so!

Now you are the body of Christ and individually members of it.

1 Corinthians 12:27

PRAY

Abba Father, help me to remember that I am part of the Body of Christ. I have brothers and sisters all over the world, yet You still call me to be the me You created me to be. Help me to function as You have planned. Help me to assist others in Your Body who cross my path. Thank You, Lord!

DECLARE

I am one in the Body of Christ!

He loves you so!

For now we see in a mirror dimly, but then face to face. Now I know in part; then I shall know fully, even as I have been fully known.

1 CORINTHIANS 13:12

PRAY

Abba Father, my vision and understanding are limited and swayed by my surroundings and circumstances. My reality is too often based on what I see and feel. When that happens, my reality and Your truth are not even close. Reality is my perception, but truth is who You are. Please help me make Your truth my reality. Thank You, Lord!

DECLARE

Today His truth will be my total reality!

He loves you so!

Be watchful, stand firm in the faith, act like men, be strong.

1 CORINTHIANS 16:13

PRAY

Strong and powerful Lord, help me not to give way to fear of what man or the enemy can do to me. Your Presence is what I need. As I lean into Your Presence, sheltered in Your mighty arms, my faith begins to expand. In You I can stand firm in faith, even when life seems overwhelming. Thank You, Lord!

DECLARE

Daily my trust, belief and faith are growing in His Presence!

He loves you so!

Blessed be the God and Father of our Lord Jesus Christ, the Father of mercies and God of all comfort.

2 CORINTHIANS 1:3

PRAY

Great Comforter, You are with me when every tear falls. You wrap Your strong arms around me and comfort my hurting heart. Open my eyes to see others the way You see me, especially those on my path who need to experience the same comfort You give me. Please use me as a comforter to others who need the hope that You give. Thank You, Lord!

DECLARE

I can comfort others with the same comfort God lavishes on me!

He loves you so!

For all the promises of God find their Yes in him. That is why it is through him that we utter our Amen to God for his glory.

2 Corinthians 1:20

PRAY

Father God, You do not stammer or stutter. You never doubt Your Word. You do not change Your mind. Your promises are not "I'm not sure" or "Maybe." Your promises are resolutely YES and AMEN! I trust confidently in Your faithfulness to utterly and perfectly complete all that You have started. I declare, "So be it—Amen!" Thank You, Lord!

DECLARE

God's promises stand firm! Yes and Amen! So be it!

He loves you so!

For we are the aroma of Christ to God among those who are being saved and among those who are perishing.

2 CORINTHIANS 2:15

PRAY

King Jesus, You victoriously pave the way before me. Defeat has no hold on me. How wonderful that I get to live from Your victory. Thank You for Your triumphant gifts of wisdom, righteousness, sanctification, redemption, freedom and victory. May I be the lingering sweet fragrance of victory in Jesus Christ to every life I encounter today. Thank You, Lord!

DECLARE

The aroma of Christ's victory pours through me!

He loves you so!

You yourselves are our letter of recommendation, written on our hearts, to be known and read by all.

2 CORINTHIANS 3:2

PRAY

Holy Spirit, thank You for Your Presence living in me. You have written the details of my life as a love letter. Mold me into the vessel that You created and called me to be. May my life be an open letter to all I meet so that they see You and want to know, believe and understand that You are love. You are God! Thank You, Lord!

DECLARE

I am God's living love letter to the world!

He loves you so!

Now the Lord is the Spirit, and where the Spirit of the Lord is, there is freedom.

2 CORINTHIANS 3:17

PRAY

Father God, thank You for those who have proclaimed with their lives that the price of freedom has been paid in full. And thank You for Jesus' blood, which paid the price to release me from the bondage of sin. I pray that You get everything You paid for. I pray to live a life worth the Price You paid! Thank You, Lord!

DECLARE

An exorbitant price was paid for me because God declared that I am worth it!

He loves you so!

And we all, with unveiled face, beholding the glory of the Lord, are being transformed into the same image from one degree of glory to another. For this comes from the Lord who is the Spirit.

2 CORINTHIANS 3:18

PRAY

Abba Father, You alone are the One who gives Your Holy Spirit in power and without measure or limit, making me brand new. You always have more for me. Help me never to be complacent or content staying where I am with You. Change me and transform me from glory to glory as I walk in Your Presence. Thank You, Lord!

DECLARE

I am being changed—transformed into the very image of King Jesus!

He loves you so!

For God, who said, "Let light shine out of darkness," has shone in our hearts to give the light of the knowledge of the glory of God in the face of Jesus Christ.

2 CORINTHIANS 4:6

PRAY

Holy Spirit, help me to work with You to give the world a clearer picture of who You are and how You move. May there be no hindrance or deterrent in me that blocks Your illuminating Light. No darkness can hide Your Light. I pray that Your Presence living in me shines Your goodness and glory brightly through me. Thank You, Lord!

DECLARE

God's brilliant Light illuminates the world through me!

He loves you so!

We are afflicted in every way, but not crushed; perplexed, but not driven to despair; persecuted, but not forsaken; struck down, but not destroyed.

2 CORINTHIANS 4:8–9

PRAY

Almighty God, Your perfect Word declares that I can never be completely wrecked or destroyed by the circumstances of my life. There is always hope, even when the trials get harder and deeper. My hope is anchored to the solid Rock of Yahweh. Father, work through me to display Your resurrection power, which gives hope to others. Thank You, Lord!

DECLARE

Yahweh firmly anchors me in the throes of the storm!

He loves you so!

We don't focus our attention on what is seen but on what is unseen. For what is seen is temporary, but the unseen realm is eternal.

2 CORINTHIANS 4:18 TPT

PRAY

Holy Spirit, so often the focus of my attention is on what I can see. I fool myself into believing that those things will last forever. Please give me vision beyond what is seen, to set my gaze fully with faith upon eternity and those things that have lasting Kingdom impact. Give me spiritual eyes to see into the unseen realm, where You dwell. Thank You, Lord!

DECLARE

My attention is focused on God's eternal Kingdom!

He loves you so!

Therefore, we are ambassadors for Christ, God making his appeal through us. We implore you on behalf of Christ, be reconciled to God.

2 CORINTHIANS 5:20

PRAY

Father God, it is a blessed and holy calling to be Your ambassador here on earth. As Your envoy, please give me wisdom as I intentionally connect with people who do not know You. Let my words and actions reflect Your love and grace so that they will see You and want to enter into a relationship with You. Thank You, Lord!

DECLARE

I am God's ambassador, releasing peace
and reconciliation everywhere I go!

He loves you so!

For our sake he made him to be sin who knew no sin, so that in him we might become the righteousness of God.

2 CORINTHIANS 5:21

PRAY

Abba Father, I humbly acknowledge that I can do nothing to earn Your forgiveness and mercy. I have tried so hard and for so long to feel worthy of the price that was paid for me. No more! I choose to live thanking You for Your marvelous gift of grace and for making me righteous through Your precious Son, Jesus. Thank You, Lord!

DECLARE

No more stress or striving! I have been made righteous!

He loves you so!

For you know the grace of our Lord Jesus Christ, that though he was rich, yet for your sake he became poor, so that you by his poverty might become rich.

2 CORINTHIANS 8:9

PRAY

King Jesus, You left the riches of heaven to walk this earth for me. You stripped Yourself of Your royal robe to wear a carpenter's tunic. You threw off Your royal crown to bear the weight of twisted thorn branches. Thank You, Lord, for Your sacrifice on my behalf. Lead me to follow You willingly and wholeheartedly. Thank You, Lord!

DECLARE

My life must be lived worthy of the price paid for me!

He loves you so!

We destroy arguments and every lofty opinion raised against the knowledge of God, and take every thought captive to obey Christ.

2 CORINTHIANS 10:5

PRAY

Lord, help me not to get lazy and lethargic, letting my thoughts run amok. I need intention and resolve to take the stance of a warrior against the arguments and opinions that come against Your character and Word. Change the way that I think; renew my mind. Remove all worldly views and replace them with the true knowledge of You. Thank You, Lord!

DECLARE

Today I will take every thought captive that is contrary to the knowledge of God!

He loves you so!

But he said to me, "My grace is sufficient for you, for my power is made perfect in weakness." Therefore I will boast all the more gladly of my weaknesses, so that the power of Christ may rest upon me.

2 CORINTHIANS 12:9

PRAY

All-powerful Lord, when I feel unable to move forward or when I have no idea of what to do, Your grace washes over me. Help me to live this day in the power of the Holy Spirit instead of being consumed by my weaknesses. Thank You for Your gift of grace that is sufficient and makes Your power perfect in and through me. Thank You, Lord!

DECLARE

God uses my weaknesses to display His mighty power!

He loves you so!

For he was crucified in weakness, but lives by the power of God. For we also are weak in him, but in dealing with you we will live with him by the power of God.

2 CORINTHIANS 13:4

PRAY

Lord, I know that whatever comes my way will be filtered through Your sovereign hand. You will not let anything come close to me that You are not already working for my good and empowering me to face. Please be with me and sustain me through Your power and grace. In this power, I will rest and rejoice. Thank You, Lord!

DECLARE

I live with Christ in the power of God!

He loves you so!

For am I now seeking the approval of man, or of God? Or am I trying to please man? If I were still trying to please man, I would not be a servant of Christ.

GALATIANS 1:10

PRAY

Precious Lord, so often I fall into the "pleasing people" trap and seek the approval of others before I seek to please You. You—You alone are the One I want to please. Please forgive me when I look to the approval of people. Strengthen me to be sure my words and actions are pleasing in Your sight. Thank You, Lord!

DECLARE

Today I will seek to please my King above all else!

He loves you so!

For freedom Christ has set us free; stand firm therefore, and do not submit again to a yoke of slavery.

GALATIANS 5:1

PRAY

Lord God, You are the ultimate Freedom Fighter. You broke off my yoke of slavery forever. You made me to live free, and You will settle for nothing less. Thank You for providing the way for me to live out the freedom You bought. Help me to walk in Your perfect freedom every day and release it everywhere I go. Thank You, Lord!

DECLARE

I am created to live in and release freedom!

He loves you so!

But I say, walk by the Spirit, and you will not gratify the desires of the flesh.

GALATIANS 5:16

PRAY

Precious Lord, it is a humbling reality that I cannot live a life of faith in my own strength. My human strength is weakness at best. The Holy Spirit provides the perfect strength I need to walk the walk, in true faith. It is freeing truth to know that through Your grace, You equip me for every situation I face! Thank You, Lord!

DECLARE

I am strengthened to walk the walk
through the Holy Spirit!

He loves you so!

For the desires of the flesh are against the Spirit, and the desires of the Spirit are against the flesh, for these are opposed to each other, to keep you from doing the things you want to do.

GALATIANS 5:17

PRAY

Gentle God, far too often my desires wrestle against Your perfect plan. Lord God, strengthen me today through Your Holy Spirit so that I do not give in to my flesh and its desires, which are contrary to the Spirit. Instead, may I do only those things that please You, for those are the things I want to do! Thank You, Lord!

DECLARE

My true heart's desire is the perfect will of God!

He loves you so!

≡ If we live by the Spirit, let us also keep in step with the Spirit.

GALATIANS 5:25

PRAY

Loving Father, how easy it is to react in the flesh when I am disappointed or frustrated. Emotions seem to unexpectedly take over me. Holy Spirit, please fill me fully so that I may walk by Your power. May I live in such a way that my words, attitudes and actions today will reflect Your grace and truth. Thank You, Lord!

DECLARE

I live by the Spirit and keep in step with Him!

He loves you so!

And let us not grow weary of doing good, for in due season we will reap, if we do not give up.

GALATIANS 6:9

PRAY

Lord, I confess that when I look at all that is going on in the world and things that haven't happened yet, I get so tired. Please remind my heart and mind that You never give up. You are always working. You are not done yet, and You have perfect timing. Give me the strength, love and grace to keep my eyes focused on You and to keep following hard after You. Thank You, Lord!

DECLARE

Exhaustion will not deter me from reaping a great harvest!

He loves you so!

He chose us in him before the foundation of the world,
that we should be holy and blameless before him.

EPHESIANS 1:4

PRAY

*Abba Father, Daddy, thank You that You have
hand-picked me. You had Your eye on me from
the beginning of time. I am alive in every way
because of Your great love. Help me to live in the
knowledge and the truth that You have chosen
me. You created and called me for Your divine
purposes. Thank You, Lord!*

DECLARE

I am chosen from the beginning of time to live
holy and blameless before my Father!

He loves you so!

He predestined us for adoption to himself as sons through Jesus Christ, according to the purpose of his will.

EPHESIANS 1:5

PRAY

Almighty Creator, oh, the pure wonder and joy of being fully accepted, just as I am! From before the foundation of the world, You wanted me and purposed me to be Your child. You have a perfect plan for me. Thank You, Abba Father, for freely lavishing Your love on me and for embracing me in Your everlasting arms because of Jesus. Thank You, Lord!

DECLARE

I am adopted and declared to be the
dearly loved child of God!

He loves you so!

Throughout the coming ages we will be the visible display of the infinite, limitless riches of his grace and kindness, which was showered upon us in Jesus Christ.

EPHESIANS 2:7 TPT

PRAY

Holy Spirit, You are alive and active today. You are working and moving in the world right now. Help me to truly comprehend, embrace and maximize the surpassing riches of Your Presence, grace and power. I pray that You are free to work in and through my daily moments to be a demonstration of Your immeasurable and unlimited mercy and kindness. Thank You, Lord!

DECLARE

I am created to boldly and visibly display
God's grace and kindness every day!

He loves you so!

For we are his workmanship, created in Christ Jesus for good works, which God prepared beforehand, that we should walk in them.

EPHESIANS 2:10

PRAY

Father God, You are my Creator. You are the Author of my life. You are the Artist, and I am Your masterpiece. You formed me and wove me together. You created me on purpose for Your purpose, for the works that You have already written in Your book. Help me to walk in those works as You have prepared them. Thank You, Lord!

DECLARE

With great joy and for His purpose,
God created and formed me!

He loves you so!

So then you are no longer strangers and aliens, but you are fellow citizens with the saints and members of the household of God.

EPHESIANS 2:19

PRAY

Lord, how incredible it is to know that because Jesus faced the ultimate rejection on my behalf, I am completely accepted. I am welcomed without hesitation into a relationship with You. When I feel alone, help me to remember that I am Your child. I am not left out or an outsider. I am forever part of Your family! Thank You, Lord!

DECLARE

I am completely accepted and fully welcomed into God's family!

He loves you so!

Here's the secret: The gospel of grace has made you, non-Jewish believers, into coheirs of his promise through your union with him. And you have now become members of his body—one with the Anointed One!

EPHESIANS 3:6 TPT

PRAY

King Jesus, You have made the way for me to know and experience You. I am grateful to be a child of the King of kings who is no longer on the outside looking in. I have become a co-heir of the Kingdom of God because of Your grace. As a member of Your Body, I am one with You. Thank You, Lord!

DECLARE

I am a co-heir of the Kingdom of God!

He loves you so!

Never doubt God's mighty power to work in you and accomplish all this. He will achieve infinitely more than your greatest request, your most unbelievable dream, and exceed your wildest imagination! He will outdo them all, for his miraculous power constantly energizes you.

EPHESIANS 3:20 TPT

PRAY

Holy Spirit, life with You is the greatest adventure! You enable me to do what I never thought I could do. You keep me going when I am about to stop. You strengthen me to go further and higher. You guide me, heal me, empower me, transform me, protect me and provide for me. You are exceedingly, abundantly beyond! Thank You, Lord!

DECLARE

God's power, which is exceedingly,
abundantly beyond, flows through me!

He loves you so!

And to be renewed in the spirit of your minds.

EPHESIANS 4:23

PRAY

God of all truth, free my mind from all wrong thinking. Release me from believing any lies. Bind up all thoughts that are contrary to Your will, Your way, Your character, Your Word. Renew my mind so that Your truth is my meditation all day long so that I do not fall for any of the enemy's deceptions. Thank You, Lord!

DECLARE

My mind is constantly being renewed
and is captivated by God's truth!

He loves you so!

Put on the new self, created after the likeness of God in true righteousness and holiness.

EPHESIANS 4:24

PRAY

Awesome God, because I am in Christ, all the old things of me are gone. I have been made brand-new. You have put a new heart and a new spirit in me. Remind me to daily choose to lay aside the old, corrupt self and to put on the new, You-formed me, created after Your likeness. Thank You, Lord!

DECLARE

I am not merely a sinner saved by grace;
I am a new creation! I am a saint!

He loves you so!

Be angry and do not sin; do not let the sun go down on your anger.

EPHESIANS 4:26

PRAY

King Jesus, You are my example of having anger but not allowing it to be all-consuming. Give me Your wisdom to distinguish between righteous anger and unrighteous anger. Holy Spirit, please guide my emotions so that I am angered by what offends You rather than by what offends me, making the way for You to be glorified. Thank You, Lord!

DECLARE

Anger will not get the best of me; it will
bring out God's best through me!

He loves you so!

☰ Give no opportunity to the devil.

EPHESIANS 4:27

PRAY

Almighty God, reveal to me any area in which I have given the enemy an open door—an opportunity—to wreak havoc in my life. Strengthen me to slam that door shut every time he tries to open it. May I quickly recognize and reject every lie he uses. No ploy of the enemy can stand in Your Presence and power. Thank You, Lord!

DECLARE

I am liberated from giving the enemy
an open door in my life!

He loves you so!

And never let ugly or hateful words come from your mouth, but instead let your words become beautiful gifts that encourage others; do this by speaking words of grace to help them.

EPHESIANS 4:29 TPT

PRAY

Father God, words are powerful. They can change a person's moment, day or life. Let my words be Your words—words that bring life and healing. Words that encourage and strengthen. Words that impart love and mercy. Words of grace and truth that are full of divine destiny and impact eternity. Thank You, Lord!

DECLARE

My words carry influence, authority and power!

He loves you so!

Be imitators of God in everything you do, for then you will represent your Father as his beloved sons and daughters.

EPHESIANS 5:1 TPT

PRAY

Lord God, it is amazing to know that You live in me and through me. By Your power, I have been set free from the chains that bound me to flesh and to sin. Empower me to live this truth out loud, choosing to obey and honor You. I pray to be Your true representation on this earth. Thank You, Lord!

DECLARE

I represent God today by being His arms, feet, love, grace, mercy, comfort and peace to the world!

He loves you so!

Finally, be strong in the Lord and in the strength of his might.

EPHESIANS 6:10

PRAY

Lord, there is no enemy You cannot defeat. There is no captive You cannot set free. There is no sickness, no disease that You cannot heal. There is no person You cannot save. There is no brokenness You cannot bind up. There is no sin You cannot forgive. There is no relationship You cannot restore. There is no need You cannot meet. There is no devastation You cannot redeem. There is no mountain You cannot move. Thank You, Lord!

DECLARE

All things are possible for the strong, all-powerful Creator and King of all creation!

He loves you so!

Put on the whole armor of God, that you may be able to stand against the schemes of the devil.

EPHESIANS 6:11

PRAY

Almighty God, I am grateful that You have not left me defenseless against the enemy. You have given me Your full armor, which provides for my protection. You have fully equipped and outfitted me with everything I need to withstand the attacks of the enemy. You are with me in every battle, protecting me and fighting for me. Thank You, Lord!

DECLARE

God has given me His full armor, and I can stand against the enemy's plans!

He loves you so!

In all circumstances take up the shield of faith, with which you can extinguish all the flaming darts of the evil one.

EPHESIANS 6:16

PRAY

King Jesus, through You I am equipped to overcome the enemy's attacks because You have provided a shield of faith as one of my weapons of war. Help me to hold the shield in strength and hope. In every circumstance, I will raise it against all arrows of accusation. I am fully protected and will see every flaming lie extinguished. Thank You, Lord!

DECLARE

I have a shield of faith that will not fail!

He loves you so!

Embrace the power of salvation's full deliverance, like a helmet to protect your thoughts from lies. And take the mighty razor-sharp Spirit-sword of the spoken Word of God.

EPHESIANS 6:17 TPT

PRAY

Father God, my Creator, I want to live out my true identity: Who You created me to be. Who You paid the highest price for me to be. I am who You say I am. Crush! Demolish any lies that stand in the way so that I embrace and live out the truth of who You say I am. You deserve to receive all You purchased on the cross. Thank You, Lord!

DECLARE

Lies are exposed and destroyed in the light of God's Truth!

He loves you so!

And I am sure of this, that he who began a good work in you will bring it to completion at the day of Jesus Christ.

PHILIPPIANS 1:6

PRAY

Holy Spirit, take over my life more and more. I need Your strength to pry my fingers from things I am holding on to that keep me from truly living out loud all You created me for. I don't want to miss one part of Your good plan because I am stubborn or controlling. I want to partner with You so that the good work Jesus began in me will be brought to completion. Thank You, Lord!

DECLARE

The good work that Jesus has begun in me, He will bring to completion!

He loves you so!

≡ For to me to live is Christ, and to die is gain.

PHILIPPIANS 1:21

PRAY

Lord God, You are my life. I ask for more—more of You! I know there is so much more of You that can pour through me. Empower me to surrender more of my life to You so that all the small, hidden places of my life will become a fountain of Your living and active Presence! Thank You, Lord!

DECLARE

More of God's living and active Presence flows through me!

He loves you so!

Complete my joy by being of the same mind, having the same love, being in full accord and of one mind.

PHILIPPIANS 2:2

PRAY

Lord, on my own I am not able to love enough; show me how to love like You. Love is a verb, not a mere feeling. Love is not love until it is put into action. Help me not to just survive life, but to live out loud Your love through understanding, kindness and gentleness. Love others through me. Thank You, Lord!

DECLARE

God perfectly and lavishly loves others through me!

He loves you so!

Do nothing from selfish ambition or conceit, but in humility count others more significant than yourselves.

PHILIPPIANS 2:3

PRAY

Father God, forgive me for focusing on and thinking way too much about myself. Help me to be less driven by my own ambitions or "rights." Please gently humble me, sweet Jesus, so that I genuinely honor others by Your example. Empty me out of me so I am able to treat others as greater than myself. Thank You, Lord!

DECLARE

Today I will choose humility as I honor others!

He loves you so!

For it is God who works in you, both to will and to work for his good pleasure.

PHILIPPIANS 2:13

PRAY

Lord God, Your work is crazy-wonderful! You empower, equip and enable me to be and do all that You created me for. You will fulfill every plan and purpose You have for me. Even more, You give me the desire, the passion, the "want to" to join in Your plan and purpose, all for Your glory and my delight. Thank You, Lord!

DECLARE

My dreams and heart desires are from
and for God's good pleasure!

He loves you so!

Indeed, I count everything as loss because of the surpassing worth of knowing Christ Jesus my Lord. For his sake I have suffered the loss of all things and count them as rubbish, in order that I may gain Christ.

PHILIPPIANS 3:8

PRAY

Awesome God, nothing can compare to living in Your courts and dancing before Your throne. Your Presence is the highest treasure. You are the most costly prize. Help me to truly consider anything rubbish that I may cherish. I lay it all down in order to gain more knowledge of You and experience more of Your abiding peace. Thank You, Lord!

DECLARE

Jesus is my highest prize and the treasure of my life!

He loves you so!

Not that I have already obtained this or am already perfect, but I press on to make it my own, because Christ Jesus has made me his own.

PHILIPPIANS 3:12

PRAY

Almighty Lord, I never want to live just an okay life, one that is only focused on survival. You are the God of wonders—do not let me settle for less. I want more of You. Please help me to keep pressing on to have a deeper relationship with You. When life feels mundane, infuse me with Your strength, energy and creativity. Thank You, Lord!

DECLARE

I am pressing in for all that God has more in store for me!

He loves you so!

One thing I do: forgetting what lies behind and straining forward to what lies ahead.

PHILIPPIANS 3:13

PRAY

Lord God, how often I let my past become a barrier to the good future I am promised with You. Help me move beyond my past failures and even my achievements whenever they are holding me back from what lies ahead. Please turn my past into a springboard that propels me forward and further in You. Thank You, Lord!

DECLARE

My past—forget about it! I am reaching for what is ahead!

He loves you so!

I press on toward the goal for the prize of the upward call of God in Christ Jesus.

PHILIPPIANS 3:14

PRAY

Father God, infuse me with the truth of who You say I am so that I can move forward confidently. Sometimes the things I have done in the past sneak up and torment me. Give me the strength to let go of the past and to run straight toward You and follow the call You have for me. Thank You, Lord!

DECLARE

People and circumstances will not hold me back; I am pressing forward in God!

He loves you so!

Be cheerful with joyous celebration in every season of life.
Let joy overflow, for you are united with the Anointed One!

PHILIPPIANS 4:4 TPT

PRAY

Almighty God, I lift my hands in ecstatic praise because You have chosen me to live at this time on Your kingdom calendar and on this side of Your precious cross. Increase my ability to choose to be thankful every day by increasing my capacity to see everything that You have ordained and opened up to me. Thank You, Lord!

DECLARE

My joy overflows because I am united with Jesus!

He loves you so!

Let gentleness be seen in every relationship, for our Lord is ever near.

PHILIPPIANS 4:5 TPT

PRAY

Holy Spirit, thank You for Your Presence, which is always near me. Wherever I am, You are there. I carry and release Your Presence with every step that I take. May those around me know and experience that even one moment in Your Presence will transform their lives and will spoil them from accepting any sad substitution. Thank You, Lord!

DECLARE

A great spoiling of the Holy Spirit is at hand! The Lord is near!

He loves you so!

Do not be anxious about anything, but in everything by prayer and supplication with thanksgiving let your requests be made known to God.

PHILIPPIANS 4:6

PRAY

Heavenly Father, You want me to bring everything that is going on in my life to You. You do not want me to keep anything from You. Nothing is too big, and nothing is too small for me to bring. Infuse me with the joy, the wonder, the power, the privilege and the peace of a life of prayer. Thank You, Lord!

DECLARE

I will thank the Lord, as my life, through prayer, rises up to His throne!

He loves you so!

Finally, brothers, whatever is true, whatever is honorable, whatever is just, whatever is pure, whatever is lovely, whatever is commendable, if there is any excellence, if there is anything worthy of praise, think about these things.

PHILIPPIANS 4:8

PRAY

Sovereign God, let my mind be filled to overflowing with the things of You. All those things that are true, honorable, right, pure, lovely, praiseworthy and excellent, let those be in my thoughts. When any unworthy thought comes, help me immediately to recognize it and reject it. Strengthen me to push out the unworthy so that Your worthy thoughts are in the forefront of my mind. Thank You, Lord!

DECLARE

My thoughts and words are becoming the supernatural thoughts and words of God's Kingdom!

He loves you so!

≡ I have learned in whatever situation I am to be content.

PHILIPPIANS 4:11

PRAY

Lord God, so often I find myself struggling and striving for more, better and other. By Your Spirit, help me to step into Your rest and contentment today. I choose to press on to walk in victory. Whatever lies ahead, I am content in the knowledge that You are with me. You supply Your all-sufficient strength. I will be still and allow You to be You, Lord! Thank You, Lord!

DECLARE

Because I know the One who holds my
future, I am content to rest!

He loves you so!

I can do all things through him who strengthens me.

PHILIPPIANS 4:13

PRAY

Almighty God, You stretched out the expanse of the heavens. You carved out the depths of the seas. You raised Jesus from the grave. There is nothing that You cannot do. I want to live in the promise that because of the strength You give, I can do whatever is before me. Help me to walk through this day in faith, strengthened by Your power and awesome might. Thank You, Lord!

DECLARE

I can do all things through Christ who is my strength!

He loves you so!

Walk in a manner worthy of the Lord, fully pleasing to him: bearing fruit in every good work and increasing in the knowledge of God.

COLOSSIANS 1:10

PRAY

Lord God, today I need Your help to walk in a way that is worthy of Your name. Help me to be fully pleasing to you by the choices I make and the answers I give. I want to bear much fruit for You, today and every day. May I be about good works and may my knowledge of You increase throughout the day. Thank You, Lord!

DECLARE

Today I will walk in a manner that is worthy of the name of Jesus!

He loves you so!

He has delivered us from the domain of darkness and transferred us to the kingdom of his beloved Son.

COLOSSIANS 1:13

PRAY

Father God, I pray to truly embrace the great transfer You have provided for me through Your Son, Jesus. Cause my heart to beat in sync with Your heart. Move me from working for Your favor to working from Your favor. May I rest in the truth that I cannot do anything to cause You to love me less or more. Thank You, Lord!

DECLARE

I have been transferred to the Kingdom of Jesus!

He loves you so!

He has now reconciled in his body of flesh by his death, in order to present you holy and blameless and above reproach before him.

COLOSSIANS 1:22

PRAY

Gracious and merciful Lord, how wonderful to know that before You I am above reproach! You see me through the blood of Christ, seated in Christ, in the heavenly places, holy and regaled in the beauty of holiness. Please strengthen me to resist the lies of the enemy that would hold me prisoner to the past. Thank You, Lord!

DECLARE

The truth is I am blameless and holy before God!

He loves you so!

Let the word of Christ dwell in you richly, teaching and admonishing one another in all wisdom, singing psalms and hymns and spiritual songs, with thankfulness in your hearts to God.

COLOSSIANS 3:16

PRAY

Lord God, Author of all truth, You have given me the gift of Your Word. It contains Your wisdom, knowledge and understanding. Through it, You guide and encourage me. Help me to crave it. Show me how to apply it. Embolden me to walk in it every moment of every day. May Your truth become my first reaction and response. Thank You, Lord!

DECLARE

The words of Christ richly live in me and flow through me!

He loves you so!

Put your heart and soul into every activity you do, as though you are doing it for the Lord himself and not merely for others.

COLOSSIANS 3:23 TPT

PRAY

Lord God, may I understand and see that every part of my life has Your divine purpose; it is a sacred calling from You. Ministry—serving You—is not allocated just to a building or to certain hours of the week. You are never that limited. Permeate every area of my life to bring light and life to the world. Thank You, Lord!

DECLARE

I do not need to work for God's approval;
I get to live from His approval!

He loves you so!

Just as we have been approved by God to be entrusted with the gospel, so we speak, not to please man, but to please God who tests our hearts.

1 THESSALONIANS 2:4

PRAY

Lord God, I am humbled and grateful that You chose to entrust the Good News to me. Please give me a teachable spirit so that I learn from my mistakes of focusing on what someone else thinks instead of Your desires. Test my heart to find any area where I need correction and redirection. As You bring those areas to light, help me to change course and follow You. Thank You, Lord!

DECLARE

I am approved and entrusted by God
to share the Good News!

He loves you so!

For the Lord himself will descend from heaven with a cry of command, with the voice of an archangel, and with the sound of the trumpet of God. And the dead in Christ will rise first.

1 THESSALONIANS 4:16

PRAY

Father God, please give me the courage and strength to live righteously and boldly because King Jesus is returning soon. One day the eastern sky will split wide open, and I will see Him face to face. I pray to be Your effective vessel to spread the truth of Your Word so others have the opportunity to know You. Thank You, Lord!

DECLARE

My testimony of Jesus' return is needed today!

He loves you so!

≡ Rejoice always.

1 THESSALONIANS 5:16

PRAY

Lord Jesus, I do not want the rocks to cry out in my place. That is not what they were created for. Rejoicing in You is my privilege and honor. Like a spring of refreshing water, fill me to bubble over with joy and gladness—rejoicing in You always. You alone are worthy to be given all honor, glory and praise! Thank You, Lord!

DECLARE

The rocks will not cry out in my place—I
will rejoice today and always!

He loves you so!

We always pray for you, that our God may make you worthy of his calling and may fulfill every resolve for good and every work of faith by his power.

2 THESSALONIANS 1:11

PRAY

Almighty Lord, today I resolve to fulfill every good work You have laid out for me. Please pour Your Spirit into me so that I am worthy and adequate for the calling You have on my life. I believe Your favor rests on me. It opens doors and opportunities that I didn't even know I desired. May Your Spirit work through me so that the name of the Lord Jesus may be glorified. Thank You, Lord!

DECLARE

God has made me worthy of His calling,
and I will fulfill every good work!

He loves you so!

The saying is trustworthy and deserving of full acceptance, that Christ Jesus came into the world to save sinners, of whom I am the foremost.

1 TIMOTHY 1:15

PRAY

Lord God, when I was utterly lost in sin, completely unworthy and desperate, You intentionally came for me and lifted me up. My total dependence rests entirely on You and Your unending love and amazing grace. Help me to live a life that humbly considers and acknowledges that You are my only Source. You have made me worthy. Thank You, Lord!

DECLARE

Even while I was still a sinner, Jesus saw me
as worthy and came to set me free!

He loves you so!

≡ Fight the good fight, keeping faith and a good conscience.

1 TIMOTHY 1:18–19 NASB 1995

PRAY

Lord God, help me to hold firm to my faith as I fight Your good fight. I want to rely on the truth that You are my Strength and my Shield. Please guard and protect my mind and heart from Satan's binding lies. May I be continually full of Your truth so that I remain focused on You. Thank You, Lord!

DECLARE

I am created to be a warrior whom God works through to reveal His Kingdom!

He loves you so!

For God gave us a spirit not of fear but of power and love and self-control.

2 TIMOTHY 1:7

PRAY

Abba Father, may I never live ashamed of Your Gospel of truth. I know it offers Your power of salvation to everyone who believes. I believe, Lord! Help me to stand strong in my faith, no matter what is happening, remembering that You have not given me a spirit of timidity, but of power and love and discipline. Thank You, Lord!

DECLARE

I am infused with the spirit of power, love and self-control!

He loves you so!

Who saved us and called us to a holy calling, not because of our works but because of his own purpose and grace, which he gave us in Christ Jesus before the ages began.

2 TIMOTHY 1:9

PRAY

Lord God, thank You that You make me more than adequate and able to do the work You created and called me to do. On my own, I can do nothing of any value, but with You, I am highly equipped and prepared. Help me to know, deep in my heart, spirit and soul, that You are the only One to whom I must answer. Thank You, Lord!

DECLARE

Through God's grace and purpose, I am equipped and prepared to accomplish great things!

He loves you so!

≡ If we are faithless, he remains faithful.

2 TIMOTHY 2:13

PRAY

Loving Father, I thank You that You care about everything that I care about, everything that concerns me. You will be faithful to provide and protect me even when I falter. Every promise You declare will come about. Please stop me when I have anxious thoughts or begin to worry instead of trusting You with my todays and all of my tomorrows. Thank You, Lord!

DECLARE

All of my days are held in my faithful God's loving hands!

He loves you so!

Do your best to present yourself to God as one approved, a worker who has no need to be ashamed, rightly handling the word of truth.

2 TIMOTHY 2:15

PRAY

Lord God, You alone are worthy of all my worship, my adoration, my affection, my praise and my service. I give this day and every day to You. Infuse me with Your Word and creativity to make You conspicuous and visible. Show me how to use my time, my words and my life for Your glory, honor and praise. Thank You, Lord!

DECLARE

I am God's worker, and my words and
my actions make Him known!

He loves you so!

Therefore, if anyone cleanses himself from what is dishonorable, he will be a vessel for honorable use, set apart as holy, useful to the master of the house, ready for every good work.

2 TIMOTHY 2:21

PRAY

Lord God, I cry out to You to pour out Your Spirit on my life. I desire to be a usable vessel for Your honor. Cleanse and renew my mind, purging any thoughts and actions that are unworthy of You. Cleanse me from the inside out. Sanctify me so that I am fit for Your use. Thank You, Lord!

DECLARE

I am cleaned, renewed and sanctified to be God's vessel!

He loves you so!

But as for you, continue in what you have learned and have firmly believed, knowing from whom you learned it.

2 TIMOTHY 3:14

PRAY

Lord God, You alone are the only wellspring of knowledge and understanding. Help me to be resolute in living the Truth I believe and remaining in it daily. I thank You and pray for those who have answered Your call and have been faithful to teach Your living truth, the Gospel. Bless them for all they are doing. Thank You, Lord!

DECLARE

By the power of the Spirit, I will continue in what I have learned and have firmly believed!

He loves you so!

For the word of God is living and active, sharper than any two-edged sword, piercing to the division of soul and of spirit, of joints and of marrow, and discerning the thoughts and intentions of the heart.

HEBREWS 4:12

PRAY

Lord God, Your Word is alive and active because You are alive and active. Your Word exposes everything that is not of You and also brings wholeness and life. Holy Spirit, please use the Word to conform me to the image of Christ so I can be a conduit, flowing Your goodness into the lives of others. Thank You, Lord!

DECLARE

My merciful God is not done with me yet!

He loves you so!

For we do not have a high priest who is unable to sympa-
thize with our weaknesses, but one who in every respect
has been tempted as we are, yet without sin.

HEBREWS 4:15

PRAY

*Lord God, some days I feel so inadequate and
ill-equipped. Too weak to move forward. Thank
You for reminding me that Jesus understands exactly how I feel. Jesus knows what it is like to live
on this earth. He has walked through the same
chaos. Through it all, He offers the mercy and
grace I so desperately need. Thank You, Lord!*

DECLARE

The King of kings knows and understands me!

He loves you so!

We have this as a sure and steadfast anchor of the soul, a hope that enters into the inner place behind the curtain.

HEBREWS 6:19

PRAY

Almighty Lord, the circumstances of my day can rise and fall without warning. Confusion or anxiety can wash over me like crashing waves. Even though I cannot predict the day, I do know You intimately. You are unchanging and a true foundation. You are my sure and steadfast anchor of hope. Hold me close to You. Thank You, Lord!

DECLARE

I am secure and anchored to God, my Great Hope!

He loves you so!

Consequently, he is able to save to the uttermost those who draw near to God through him, since he always lives to make intercession for them.

HEBREWS 7:25

PRAY

Father God, teach me to continually draw near to You. When I do not know how to pray, and when I cannot think of the words to say, You understand the groanings of my heart. Help me to remember that Jesus is continually interceding on my behalf. You hear Him, and You also hear the cry of my heart. Thank You, Lord!

DECLARE

Jesus prays for me and is able to save me!

He loves you so!

Now we are brothers and sisters in God's family because of the blood of Jesus, and he welcomes us to come right into the most holy sanctuary in the heavenly realm—boldly and with no hesitation.

HEBREWS 10:19 TPT

PRAY

Abba Father, because the blood of Jesus flows over me, You have flung wide the door for me to come boldly and confidently into Your throne room, with no fear or hesitation. You welcome me with open arms. As a child of the King, I have a birthright with full access, along with all my brothers and sisters, to Your Presence. Thank You, Lord!

DECLARE

By the blood of Jesus, I have free access
to the throne of the King!

He loves you so!

Let us draw near with a true heart in full assurance of faith, with our hearts sprinkled clean from an evil conscience and our bodies washed with pure water.

HEBREWS 10:22

PRAY

Father God, You have completely forgiven all my sin. All my failures have been wiped away. You have washed me and made me clean. Thank You for this wonderful gift! You lifted all heaviness off of me—no more weight to hold me down. Thank You for the great blessing to walk in grace and not in guilt! Thank You, Lord!

DECLARE

I can draw near to God in confidence
because He has forgiven me!

He loves you so!

But we are certainly not those who are held back by fear and perish; we are among those who have faith and experience true life!

HEBREWS 10:39 TPT

PRAY

Lord, thank You for the testimonies of those who came before me. Those who believed for the impossibilities in You. Give me dreams for the impossible that will display the wonder of You. Help me not to be fearful of what seems impossible, but to keep my eyes fixed on You. You are the Author, the Focus, the Perfecter of my faith. Thank You, Lord!

DECLARE

My impossible is where God is just getting started!

He loves you so!

Now faith is the assurance of things hoped for, the conviction of things not seen.

HEBREWS 11:1

PRAY

Precious Lord, I believe that You alone are the Almighty God and that You are the giver of my faith. You are never shocked or shaken by the events of this world. I am certain and confident that my every moment is planned and held in Your hand. I choose to live in the assurance of Your Word. Thank You, Lord!

DECLARE

I am convinced and assured by the
gift of faith God has given me!

He loves you so!

Therefore, since we are surrounded by so great a cloud of witnesses, let us also lay aside every weight, and sin which clings so closely, and let us run with endurance the race that is set before us.

HEBREWS 12:1

PRAY

Lord, I find great encouragement in knowing that so many before me have traveled faithfully and victoriously with You. I am surrounded by that great cloud of witnesses, so help me to throw off everything that hinders and the sin that so easily tangles me up in care and worry. Help me run with perseverance the race You have marked out for me. Teach me to fix my eyes on You, the Author and Perfecter of my faith. Thank You, Lord!

DECLARE

Surrounded by Your witnesses, I will persevere
and run the race with endurance!

He loves you so!

Looking to Jesus, the founder and perfecter of our faith, who for the joy that was set before him endured the cross, despising the shame, and is seated at the right hand of the throne of God.

HEBREWS 12:2

PRAY

Lord, please open my eyes to what You want to accomplish in me and through me during difficult circumstances. Help me to resist the temptation to look for easy ways out of my trials, for I know trying to maneuver and manipulate things on my own will only make the situation worse. Help me to see You in all things. Thank You, Lord!

DECLARE

Jesus is the Author and Perfecter of my faith in all circumstances!

He loves you so!

Therefore let us be grateful for receiving a kingdom that cannot be shaken, and thus let us offer to God acceptable worship, with reverence and awe.

HEBREWS 12:28

PRAY

King Jesus, thank You for making the way for me to be part of Your immovable and unshakeable Kingdom. Things in this world are trembling and quaking all around me, but I live in a kingdom that is firm and secure because what is eternal, unwavering and steadfast dwells within me. Help me to stand firm in every shaking circumstance. Thank You, Lord!

DECLARE

The eternal, unshakeable realities of
God's Kingdom are in me!

He loves you so!

≡ Our God is a consuming fire.

HEBREWS 12:29

PRAY

Father God, You are the Consuming Fire. I pray that You burn through my life, disrupting the way I do things and destroying any wicked way found in me. Help me to discern what You are doing so that I move out of the way and let You work freely—letting You consume whatever is in my path that is not of You. Thank You, Lord!

DECLARE

God's consuming fire burns in me and through me!

He loves you so!

≡ Jesus Christ is the same yesterday and today and forever.

HEBREWS 13:8

PRAY

Jesus, You healed diseases, You cast out oppression, You gave sight to the blind, You made the deaf to hear, You restored the broken, You loved the outcast, You set captives free, You defeated enemy armies, You raised the dead back to life, You brought water from the rock and You made a way where there seemed to be no way. You will do it all again! You are the same yesterday, TODAY and forever. Thank You, Lord!

DECLARE

God is never changing—He is always the same!

He loves you so!

Through him then let us continually offer up a sacrifice of praise to God, that is, the fruit of lips that acknowledge his name.

HEBREWS 13:15

PRAY

Abba Father, I want praise to You to always be on my lips. Let my adoration be a continual and pleasing sacrifice before Your throne. For all You have done and continue to do, I worship and adore You. I want to worship You with every ounce of my being. You alone are worthy to be adored! Thank You, Lord!

DECLARE

Praise and worship of God is my natural language!

He loves you so!

If any of you lacks wisdom, let him ask God, who gives generously to all without reproach, and it will be given him.

JAMES 1:5

PRAY

Lord God, Your wisdom is like no other's. Help me to walk in that kind of wisdom—pure in thought and intent, peaceable, gentle, open to reason, merciful and bearing good fruit. Please give me Your wisdom to find Your true healing and freedom. I ask today for Your wisdom, counsel and direction to navigate the path that is laid out before me. Thank You, Lord!

DECLARE

God imparts His divine wisdom to me,
and I get to deliver it to others!

He loves you so!

Blessed is the man who remains steadfast under trial, for when he has stood the test he will receive the crown of life, which God has promised to those who love him.

JAMES 1:12

PRAY

Lord, at times, the trials of my life are so discouraging and disheartening. But I know that if I stand strong in faith, You fulfill Your promise to me as Your child. Help me follow Your truth carefully, passing every test, so that one day I will stand before You unashamed to receive the crown of life, which You have promised to those who love You. And I do love You! Thank You, Lord!

DECLARE

I resolve to remain steadfast and immovable in any circumstance!

He loves you so!

Every good gift and every perfect gift is from above, coming down from the Father of lights, with whom there is no variation or shadow due to change.

JAMES 1:17

PRAY

Father God, thank You for the joy of knowing that I can come to You with each and every request, with everything I need. I will trust Your answers and Your ways, even if they are not exactly what I pray for, because I know that You will give me what is for my best. You are for me! Thank You, Lord!

DECLARE

God is unchangeable Light, and He
gives good and perfect gifts!

He loves you so!

But the one who looks into the perfect law, the law of liberty, and perseveres, being no hearer who forgets but a doer who acts, he will be blessed in his doing.

JAMES 1:25

PRAY

Father God, help me to see into Your Word and to persevere in it. My desire is not only to listen to Your Word, but also to act on Your Word. I will put feet to the pavement and muscle to serving my God and others. If I only listen and do not obey, I just cheat myself. Thank You, Lord!

DECLARE

I hear God's Word, and I act on God's Word!

He loves you so!

The Scripture was fulfilled that says, "Abraham believed God, and it was counted to him as righteousness"—and he was called a friend of God.

JAMES 2:23

PRAY

Abba Father, my heart and my soul cry out and crave an intimate relationship with You—my Creator and Savior. You created me, and You desire to have an intimate relationship with me. The truth that You call me Your friend thrills my whole being. This living, active friendship with You brings such joy to my every moment. Thank You, Lord!

DECLARE

I am the friend of God! God is my Friend!

He loves you so!

But he gives more grace. Therefore it says, "God opposes the proud but gives grace to the humble."

JAMES 4:6

PRAY

Precious Lord, pride is such a sly thing. It sneaks up on me unnoticed. Guard my heart and mind against the lie that I am safe from being prideful. Release me from thinking too highly or too lowly of myself. Free my thoughts of thinking of myself too much. May humility that glorifies You alone be evident in my daily life. Thank You, Lord!

DECLARE

Humility keeps me living in truth and glorifies God!

He loves you so!

≡ The prayer of a righteous person is powerful and effective.

JAMES 5:16 NIV

PRAY

Almighty God, in You, it is impossible for me to pray and for nothing to happen. My eyes may not see it. My ears may not hear it. But my words have reached the throne room and touched the heart of the Ancient of Days. Thank You that the power of prayer is not in me, the one who prays, but in YOU, the One who hears! Thank You, Lord!

DECLARE

My prayers are effective and powerful
to accomplish God's purposes!

He loves you so!

Whoever brings back a sinner from his wandering will save his soul from death and will cover a multitude of sins.

JAMES 5:20

PRAY

Father God, You sent the Holy Spirit and others to bring me back from my aimless wandering with You. Help me now to pay it forward because You love everyone and want each person to receive Your gift of salvation. Give me discernment that I may be used by You to bring hope and healing into the lives of others. Protect me from hypocrisy and grow in me a spirit of gentleness and love. Thank You, Lord!

DECLARE

I am a living, walking, talking illustration of God's love!

He loves you so!

We are reborn into a perfect inheritance that can never perish, never be defiled, and never diminish. It is promised and preserved forever in the heavenly realm for you.

1 PETER 1:4 TPT

PRAY

Almighty Lord, You are great in mercy and lavish in love. All Your precious promises are "yes" through Jesus Christ. The "promises" of this world are like shifting shadows—here one moment and gone the next. You are the only absolute guarantee in all of life. Help me cling to the only thing I can never lose—You! Thank You, Lord!

DECLARE

My eternity is grounded and secure in Jesus Christ!

He loves you so!

So that the tested genuineness of your faith—more precious than gold that perishes though it is tested by fire—may be found to result in praise and glory and honor at the revelation of Jesus Christ.

1 Peter 1:7

PRAY

God, it can be so hard when my faith is tested. I think I might fail the test. But it is in the testing that I discover my faith is genuine. I cry out to You: Help my unbelief! Give me opportunities to grow my faith! Show me the beautiful faith that You are growing through my difficulties and trials. It is all evidence that You are working the circumstances out for my good and for Your glory. Thank You, Lord!

DECLARE

My faith is tested and has been proved genuine!

He loves you so!

You have been born again, not of perishable seed but of imperishable, through the living and abiding word of God.

1 PETER 1:23

PRAY

Lord, thank You for sending Your eternal Word, which has all power and authority to heal me, deliver me, guide me and free me. I praise You for the knowledge and truth that I have been reborn through Your Spirit and the living and abiding Word. You have made me more than enough and well-equipped for every good work You have purposed for me. Thank You, Lord!

DECLARE

I am born again through the imperishable Word of God!

He loves you so!

He himself bore our sins in his body on the tree, that we might die to sin and live to righteousness. By his wounds you have been healed.

1 PETER 2:24

PRAY

King Jesus, my blessed Redeemer, what an awesome, unspeakable gift of God—the sacrifice of You, His Son, in my place. Jesus, thank You for lifting the weight of all my sin and taking it on Yourself to carry and pay in full. Let me live every day in gratitude of Your incomprehensible and scandalous love and grace. Thank You, Lord!

DECLARE

The price has been paid in full! I am healed and redeemed!

He loves you so!

In your hearts honor Christ the Lord as holy, always being prepared to make a defense to anyone who asks you for a reason for the hope that is in you; yet do it with gentleness and respect.

1 PETER 3:15

PRAY

King Jesus, help my heart to be steadfast and true, always ready to honor and declare You by telling others of the hope that lives in me. May Your perfect words always be on my tongue, eager to give an answer for why I have such joyous hope. May I be convicted of knowing, loving and following You. Thank You, Lord!

DECLARE

The perfect words about my great hope—
Jesus!—are always on my lips!

He loves you so!

Every believer has received grace gifts, so use them to serve one another as faithful stewards of the many-colored tapestry of God's grace.

1 PETER 4:10 TPT

PRAY

Lord God, show me how I can best boldly live out the gifts and calling You have lavished on me. You have gifted me to be Your beautiful, creative blessing of grace and love in this world. Let me live out divine purpose and fulfillment in doing what You created and called me to be and to do. Thank You, Lord!

DECLARE

I am gifted by God and called to be a blessing in this world!

He loves you so!

Likewise, you who are younger, be subject to the elders. Clothe yourselves, all of you, with humility toward one another, for "God opposes the proud but gives grace to the humble."

1 PETER 5:5

PRAY

Lord, I know there is nothing that I could ever do to earn or deserve Your gift of grace. Your grace overwhelms me, flooding my soul with refreshing joy and energizing freedom. In grace, I have been covered with the royal robes of Your children. Thank You for freely lavishing grace upon grace, which is Your heart toward me. Thank You, Lord!

DECLARE

I am continually lavished in grace upon grace!

He loves you so!

Humble yourselves, therefore, under the mighty hand of
God so that at the proper time he may exalt you.

1 PETER 5:6

PRAY

*Almighty God, help me not to seek after my own
thoughts, wants and desires. Grant me humility
and patience to wait upon You and Your perfect
timing. Help me keep in mind Your eternal per-
spective when life is not going the way I think it
should. Cause me to sit under Your mighty hand
and wait upon You. Thank You, Lord!*

DECLARE

In Christ, I am positioned under the hand of
God, and I eagerly await His timing!

He loves you so!

Casting all your anxieties on him, because he cares for you.

1 PETER 5:7

PRAY

Father God, it is hard to comprehend just how much You care about me. You see every detail of my life. You know everything that concerns me, and You care about it all. Help me to more readily lay all my concerns in Your mighty hands and to leave them there, knowing that You have it all under Your control. Thank You, Lord!

DECLARE

God is in the details of my life!

He loves you so!

His divine power has granted to us all things that pertain to life and godliness, through the knowledge of him who called us to his own glory and excellence.

2 PETER 1:3

PRAY

Almighty, Wonderful God, I thank You that I am not bound by any old chains. The bonds have all been broken, and all shackles have been dropped. I am free to stand with head and hands held high. Your divine power has granted me everything I need pertaining to life and godliness. Help me to stand firm in that knowledge today. Thank You, Lord!

DECLARE

I am standing firm, filled with God's divine power and covered by His excellence!

He loves you so!

My little children, I am writing these things to you so that you may not sin. But if anyone does sin, we have an advocate with the Father, Jesus Christ the righteous.

1 JOHN 2:1

PRAY

King Jesus, I am so thankful that even though I try to do my best and not sin, when I do, You are in heaven, seated at the right hand of God, continually pleading my case before Him. You are there night and day, taking up my case, advocating for me and declaring words of life over me. Thank You, Lord!

DECLARE

My faithful and true Advocate is the perfect Lamb of God!

He loves you so!

And the world is passing away along with its desires, but whoever does the will of God abides forever.

1 JOHN 2:17

PRAY

Everlasting God, I can get so easily wrapped up in things that are fleeting. Please captivate my heart and mind so that I am not distracted or drawn away from You by things that do not matter and that lack eternal value. My deepest prayer is that You will help me to walk in Your will today. Help me to focus my vision on the things that matter to You. Thank You, Lord!

DECLARE

My eyes are fixed on the things that matter to my Father!

He loves you so!

See what kind of love the Father has given to us, that we should be called children of God; and so we are.

1 JOHN 3:1

PRAY

Lord God Almighty, Your lavish, everlasting, unshakeable love washes wonder and awe over me. No matter what comes my way, I know that You will never leave me. You will never abandon me. You will never give up on me. You will never take Your loving gaze off me. I am safe and secure in the palm of Your hand. Thank You, Lord!

DECLARE

God never takes His eyes of love off of me!

He loves you so!

Beloved, we are God's children now, and what we will be has not yet appeared; but we know that when he appears we shall be like him, because we shall see him as he is.

1 John 3:2

PRAY

King Jesus, thank You for Your willingness and love to become flesh and blood, for Your precious obedience to leave the glory of heaven in order to die in my place. You suffered for my sins. Thank You that Your very Presence—the Holy Spirit— dwells in and through me and is transforming me into Your very likeness. Thank You, Lord!

DECLARE

I am being transformed into the very image of Jesus!

He loves you so!

Little children, you are from God and have overcome them, for he who is in you is greater than he who is in the world.

1 JOHN 4:4

PRAY

Victorious Jesus, this world holds overwhelming chaos. But Your truth proclaims that You have overcome all that chaos! Help me to lean into Your victory, to take heart, to let go of all fear, to continue to hang on, to press in and to live out loud Your eternal triumph! Thank You, Lord!

DECLARE

God, the Great I Am, lives in me!

He loves you so!

Beloved, let us love one another, for love is from God, and whoever loves has been born of God and knows God.

1 JOHN 4:7

PRAY

Beautiful Lord, Your living water of love bubbles up and fills me to overflowing. Help me not to be selfish and try to contain the love for myself. I will not settle for some weak substitute that will never satisfy. I want to be a fountain of Your life-giving and life-changing love, which splashes on all around me. Thank You, Lord!

DECLARE

God's river of love flows in and overflows through me!

He loves you so!

This is love: He loved us long before we loved him. It was his love, not ours. He proved it by sending his Son to be the pleasing sacrificial offering to take away our sins.

1 JOHN 4:10 TPT

PRAY

Abba Father, I believe in Your everlasting love. You loved me before the creation of the world. Not only do I believe, I accept Your unconditional love. I trust in Your sovereign control over the circumstances of my life. I will rest in the knowledge and truth that I am loved beyond measure and that You are always trustworthy and unchanging. Thank You, Lord!

DECLARE

I know God has always loved me, and He sent Jesus to take away my sins!

He loves you so!

We have come into an intimate experience with God's love, and we trust in the love he has for us. God is love! Those who are living in love are living in God, and God lives through them.

1 JOHN 4:16 TPT

PRAY

Abba Father, how truly revolutionary it is to know and believe that You just plain, outright love me. You are not waiting for me to be good enough. Instead, You radically, unconditionally love me completely and totally just the way I am. All You desire from me is for me to want and need You. You love me wholly! Thank You, Lord!

DECLARE

I live in God's love, and His love lives through me!

He loves you so!

There is no fear in love, but perfect love casts out fear. For fear has to do with punishment, and whoever fears has not been perfected in love.

1 John 4:18

PRAY

Abba Father, help me to step toward Your loving Presence and away from all anxiety and fear. In Your perfect love, all fear vanishes. I claim and proclaim the truth of Your love over any and all fear that has been nagging me. Fear, be gone in Jesus' love! Today I choose to rest in Your arms and receive Your peace. Thank You, Lord!

DECLARE

God's perfect love casts out all fear!
Fear has no hold on me!

He loves you so!

For everyone who has been born of God overcomes the world. And this is the victory that has overcome the world—our faith.

1 JOHN 5:4

PRAY

Victorious Lord, I need to declare Your victory over some things today. Victory! The chains are broken off! The battle is over! Triumph has been gained! Jesus has won the war! My victory has been bought and paid for! Jesus leads me in triumph! I am a victor! I no longer fight for victory; I fight from victory! Thank You, Lord!

DECLARE

I live a life of faith from His victory!

He loves you so!

And this is the confidence that we have toward him, that
if we ask anything according to his will he hears us.

1 JOHN 5:14

PRAY

*Almighty Lord, You will not keep anything good
from me. You have more good for me than I know
to ask for. You delight to hear my voice, so today
I ask You, Holy Spirit, to demonstrate Your power
and righteousness through me. I have confidence
that when I ask according to Your will, You hear
me. Thank You, Lord!*

DECLARE

God always delights to hear and respond to my voice!

He loves you so!

"Jesus Christ the faithful witness, the firstborn of the dead, and the ruler of kings on earth. To him who loves us and has freed us from our sins by his blood."

REVELATION 1:5

PRAY

Lord Jesus, You are the Faithful Witness, my Advocate. You are the King of kings, the Victorious Lamb of God. You are the Almighty Living One, my Conquering Savior. You are the Risen Messiah, my Freedom Fighter. Because of You, I am free from sin and death. You alone are worthy of all the honor, glory and praise. Thank You, Lord!

DECLARE

Jesus Christ, the Faithful Witness,
has freed me from my sin!

He loves you so!

To the one who has made us to rule as a kingly priesthood to serve his God and Father—to him be glory and dominion throughout the eternity of eternities! Amen!

REVELATION 1:6 TPT

PRAY

King Jesus, through Your perfect obedience, I have gained the privilege of being a priest in the courts of the Great I Am. Because You courageously submitted to "not My will, but Yours be done," I have the honor of carrying Your Presence wherever I go. I ask that You would remind me of that truth—as a priest before You, may I represent You well. Thank You, Lord!

DECLARE

I am a royal priest in the Kingdom of the Great I Am!

He loves you so!

"I am the Alpha and the Omega," says the Lord God, "who is and who was and who is to come, the Almighty."

REVELATION 1:8

PRAY

Lord God, You are the Alpha and the Omega. You are the First and the Last. You are the Beginning and the End. There is nothing outside Your reach. You have gone before me, making the way. Help me to remember that You walk each step with me and are guarding my future. You alone are my Lord God Almighty! Thank You, Lord!

DECLARE

God, the Almighty, goes before me
and is my guard behind me!

He loves you so!

I was in the Spirit on the Lord's day, and I heard behind me a loud voice like a trumpet.

REVELATION 1:10

PRAY

Father, every day is Your day. It is imperative that I live and move and have my being in the Holy Spirit, so that wherever I go, I take You with me. Your Presence and power go with me. Help me to be aware of Your voice, whether it be loud, like a trumpet blast, or Your still, small voice. Thank You, Lord!

DECLARE

I determine to live in the Spirit today!

He loves you so!

And they sang a new song, saying, "Worthy are you to take the scroll and to open its seals, for you were slain, and by your blood you ransomed people for God from every tribe and language and people and nation."

REVELATION 5:9

PRAY

Lord, today events and circumstances are causing my heart to become discouraged. However, the preview You have given me for the end of the story leads my heart to a higher place to shout, "VICTORY!" The Worthy Lamb, slain from the beginning, now the Lion of Judah, has thwarted the plan of the enemy working against me. Thank You, Lord!

DECLARE

Victory has already been written into my story!

He loves you so!

And I heard a loud voice in heaven, saying, "Now the salvation and the power and the kingdom of our God and the authority of his Christ have come, for the accuser of our brothers has been thrown down, who accuses them day and night before our God."

REVELATION 12:10

PRAY

Lord God, thank You that my sins are absolutely forgiven, wiped out and remembered no more. My sin debt has been paid in full. Help me to cling to that perfect truth when the enemy tries to discourage and defeat me. When he comes to accuse me and attempts to remind me of my past, may I fearlessly remind him of his future. Thank You, Lord!

DECLARE

I live in the salvation, power and Kingdom of God!

He loves you so!

And they have conquered him by the blood of the Lamb and by the word of their testimony, for they loved not their lives even unto death.

REVELATION 12:11

PRAY

Glorious Lord, may I always remember and declare that there is power—Your power—in the words I speak, declare and write. The testimony You have written in me holds Your power. I pray that every word You proclaim through me will encourage, edify, motivate and build up those around me. May Your words bring abundant life to people today and to future generations. Thank You, Lord!

DECLARE

God releases life through my words—my testimony!

He loves you so!

"They will make war on the Lamb, and the Lamb will conquer them, for he is Lord of lords and King of kings, and those with him are called and chosen and faithful."

REVELATION 17:14

PRAY

Almighty God, You have already written the end of the story of the ages. Victory is imminent. Triumph is declared. The battle has been won. Because of the Lamb slain before the foundation of the world, I am on the winning side. May I live a life worthy of You saying that I am called, chosen and faithful. Thank You, Lord!

DECLARE

God says that I am called, I am chosen and I am faithful!

He loves you so!

Then I saw heaven opened, and behold, a white horse! The one sitting on it is called Faithful and True, and in righteousness he judges and makes war.

REVELATION 19:11

PRAY

Conquering King, Triumphant Lord, Victorious Redeemer! You alone are the One and Only, True, Living and Faithful God. You have been working since the beginning of time to bring Your redemption plan to its culmination. I joyously anticipate the day You split the eastern sky and I gaze upon the Rider on the white horse in final victory! Thank You, Lord!

DECLARE

My heart beats in expectation of King Jesus' return!

He loves you so!

And he who was seated on the throne said, "Behold, I am making all things new." Also he said, "Write this down, for these words are trustworthy and true."

REVELATION 21:5

PRAY

Almighty Lord, I am grateful that I don't have to wait for the calendar to change, because today You are making all things new—this very day. Your promises are not just a grand idea or a far-off hope; they are perfect. What You promise is what You will do. Help me to trust in Your perfect timing. Thank You, Lord!

DECLARE

Today is a great day for a miracle!

He loves you so!

He who testifies to these things says, "Surely I am coming soon." Amen. Come, Lord Jesus!

REVELATION 22:20

PRAY

King Jesus, my heart is expectantly counting the days until Your glorious return. Come, Lord! I see the signs of the times. Come, Lord! I sense the eternal clock is winding down. Come, Jesus! In the fullness of time, You have promised to return. Help me to look to the heavens in expectation of Your soon return. Thank You, Lord!

DECLARE

I am counting down the days until I see Him face to face!

He loves you so!

Special Invitation

As you read this book, you may have realized that you want to go deeper in your relationship with God, or that you have yet to welcome Jesus into your life and follow Him as King.

In the beginning, God created the world, and everything was good (see Genesis 1–2). But after the first humans disobeyed God, sin entered the world, which separated us from God and brought eternal death (see Genesis 3; Romans 3:23; 5:12; 6:23).

The good news is that "God so loved the world, that he gave his only Son [Jesus], that whoever believes in him should not perish but have eternal life" (John 3:16). Jesus came to earth, lived a sinless life and was crucified, receiving the punishment for our sins. He rose from the dead, defeating sin and death, and will return as King.

Will you receive Jesus as your Lord and Savior? Share your heart with God in this prayer: *Jesus, I no longer want to do things my way, and I choose to follow You as my*

Lord. Forgive me and fill me with Your Holy Spirit to live for You every day.

To discover resources to help you grow in your faith, visit

- Bible.com or the YouVersion Bible app
- Messengerx.com or the MessengerX app
- Faithful.co or the Faithful app
- Chosenbooks.com